COMMITMENT TO THE DEAD

One Woman's Journey Toward Understanding

HELEN WATERFORD

1993

RENAISSANCE HOUSE
PUBLISHERS
541 Oak Street • P.O. Box 177
Frederick, CO 80530
(303) 833-2030

Renaissance House Publishers
A Division of JENDE-HAGAN, INC.
541 Oak Street * P.O. Box 177
Frederick, CO 80530

Library of Congress Cataloging in Publication Data

Waterford, Helen, 1909-
    Commitment to the dead.
    Bibliography: p.
    1. Waterford, Helen, 1909-   . 2. Jews--
Germany (West)--Frankfurt am Main--Biography.
3. Holocaust, Jewish (1939-1945)--Personal narratives.
4. Holocaust survivors--United States--Biography.
I. Title.
DS135.G5W338   1987   940.53'15'0392404341   87-20819
ISBN: 0-939650-63-0 (Hardcover)
ISBN: 0-939650-62-2 (Paperback)

Front cover photo of Auschwitz in 1960, by Stanley Zamonski.
Back cover photo of enamel cup, so important to life in Auschwitz, by John Ayer III.

To our dear Righteous Gentile friends:

Stien and Dirk DeBoer
Gre Driessen
Rinus Hille
Bep and Ab Reusink Sr.
Gre and Piet Tjeertes
Jo Vis

who many times risked their lives
and the lives of their families,
to save us.

FOREWORD

The Holocaust, the methodically planned extermination of European Jews under the cover of World War II, has been recorded so voluminously that even its singular atrocities have become numbingly repetitious to many, except to its survivors. That does grave injustice to the cataclysm of our century, which wasn't merely a Jewish tragedy, but a failure of all humanity. It would be better if the term "Holocaust" were not commonly associated with the fate of the Jews, for that may unfairly imply that the Jews are not sufficiently concerned with the memory of the other victims. Does anyone, it is argued, light candles to commemorate the death of the gypsies, the homosexuals, or the Jehovah's Witnesses, who, with other "subhumans," were deemed unworthy to live?

"We shall never forget and we shall never forgive" is still the cry of most Jews. And who can blame them? Even hatred is a feeble response to mass extinction, and perhaps the only means of dealing with one's sorrow and fear.

As a Jewish death camp survivor, Helen Waterford is unique; she doesn't fit that common category of victim. In *Commitment to the Dead*, she has written an unsparing, honest account from her childhood in Frankfurt to the present. But despite its realism, the book contains not one word of vengeance against her oppressors. The cool reason which is the hallmark of her trenchant narrative, can be unsettling; it's almost as if she had performed an autopsy on her own life. That determination to dissect the past unemotionally sets her book apart from all other books that I have read by survivors. There is no appeal to pity or strong thread of accusation here, no exclamation of "Why me, oh God?" It's a search for meaning -- an attempt to unravel the enigma of what people can do to each other -- not a reproach to fate.

Helen Waterford and I have been lecture partners since 1980, in a joint effort to bring both sides of the Nazi experience to light. As a former fanatic adherent of Hitler and his regime, my credentials in judging her sincerity are impeccable, but I must admit that I doubted her claim that she didn't hate any of us when we first met. I know I once hated, and I still feel so ill at ease with "the other side" that I could never have done what she did; approach me, the former, deadly enemy, and offer a hand -- not of forgiveness but of understanding.

In her book, Helen follows the same motif that guides her lectures. From beginning to end, it is a "Journey Toward Understanding," not a recital of self-pity interspersed with gruesome details of torture which draw tears. Its unblinking honesty makes the book convincing as well as poignant.

A sentence in her closing paragraph, expresses her intention best: "Hatred, unending hatred, is not the seed bed from which redemption can grow. I do not wish my children and the world's children to live forever by hatred."

That is the magnanimous premise of this unique book, and the testament of an unusual, strong woman who, despite Auschwitz, still looks to the future in the unshaken belief that "deep down, men are good."

-- *Alfons Heck, 1987*

With husband Siegfried in Amsterdam, 1935.

Lecturing with former Nazi, Alfons Heck, 1980s.

PREFACE

The lilies of the valley were never more beautiful than in May of 1945. I walked out the gate at the Womens Labor Camp at Kratzau (now Chrastava) in Czechoslovakia -- FREE. I threw myself into the large field of these dainty little flowers, embraced as many as I could, overwhelmed by their sweet smell, which filled me with joy, hope, rebirth and new security.

There was no mistaking the loud, clear question: "Mr. Heck, would you have killed Mrs. Waterford if you had been ordered to do so?" In the large auditorium of Sierra High School in San Diego, more than 600 students nervously awaited the answer. Alfons Heck, ten years old when he volunteered for the Hitler Youth, ultimately became one of the highest ranking leaders of this enthusiastic group of millions of boys. Since 1980, he has been my speaking partner on a nationwide lecture circuit. Heck's answer, halting but firm, was, "Yes, I would have done so." Walking to our cars following the lecture, he expressed concern that he had hurt my feelings, but said he had told the truth. I assured him that I understood; that I could have never believed him henceforth if he had not answered truthfully.

This book is my life story, remembrances of the years of happiness, excitement, learning and growing, years of pain and sorrow, but above all, friendship and love. Please accept this report of a full life of nearly 80 years as an overstuffed basket, whose contents just tumble out. The events are recorded as logically as possible, but in all our lives, later events are connected to earlier ones if we are fortunate enough to live long. The center of my rather long life as I look back, is what I like to call *My War*. The woman of the pre- and post-war years is so different, that there seem to be three personalities in one. My three selves share one common thread: the love for life, and empathy with all that is living.

Now, in the third and last section of my life, it seems time to judge and to be judged. This part of my life began hesitantly a few years after World War II. I was 45 years old. I had created a fulfilling life, only to find it shattered, destroyed by the world around. The illusion that if we live on an island and do not disturb the clock of time, we will live happily ever after, was gone forever. I had recovered physically from my internment, and believed that my mental balance was also restored. I wished to share what I had acquired at such a terrific and painful cost; to combine my experiences with historical fact, and lay the foundation for a growing interest in this period of history, especially among the young people.

At first, few were interested or cared to listen; these events were still too recent. In retrospect, I was naive in my approach, but at no time did I abandon my goal. I continued to study and research, in order to be ready when there should be interest in what I might have to say.

While I was writing, I was reminded by a person who had been in my audience some years ago, that I had said I would never write a book. I had said that I preferred speaking engagements, for it was there that I had an opportunity to reach as many people as possible to spread my message. I had maintained that since many people read very little, the chances of making large numbers of people aware of the past, and conscious that it could happen again, are better when you talk to large audiences.

I overcame my fears of expressing myself in writing with encouragement from my publisher. The speaking engagements had to be reduced, as much as I disliked it, but who can fight aging? So a book seemed the next logical step.

I still see in the spoken word a deeper and more direct influence, but verbal communication is, admittedly, sooner forgotten. I wrote from my conviction that history must be related, from one generation to the next. I was further motivated by my respect for education, and for the written word. Finally, I wanted to give readers the chance to share a truthful report from one ordinary woman who had experienced the depths to which mankind can sink. Here, I hope, I can show that only a strong belief in one's own potential can eventually overcome all.

Certified Copy of an Entry of Marriage.

Pursuant to the Acts for the Registration of Births, Deaths, and Marriages, in England, 1836 to 1898.

Marriage SOLEMNIZED AT THE REGISTER OFFICE, in the District of WHITECHAPEL, in the County of LONDON.

Page 8

Columns No.	When Married.	Name and Surname	Age	Condition.	Rank or Profession	Residence at the time of Marriage.	Father's Name and Surname	Rank or Profession of Father.
15	Twenty fifth June 1908	Samuel Katz	26 years	Bachelor	Corn Merchant	24 Middlesex Street Whitechapel	Hirsch Katz	Bank Cashier
		Betty Nussbaum	22	Spinster	—	24 Middlesex Street Whitechapel	Abraham Nussbaum	Cattle Dealer

Married in the REGISTER OFFICE, according to the Rites and Ceremonies of the _____ by Licence, before me,

| This Marriage was solemnized between us | Samuel Katz | in the Presence of us, | A. Donner | E. Bacon — Registrar |
| | Betty Nussbaum | | L. Cohen | F. J. Jooteel — Superintendent Registrar |

I hereby Certify the above to be a True Copy of the Entry No. 15 in the **Marriage** Register, No. 51, for the said District of WHITECHAPEL.

Witness my Hand this 25th day of June 19 08.

E. _____ con. Registrar.

the said Register being legally in my custody.

The Statutory Fees payable or an ordinary certified copy of an entry in a Register of Births, Deaths, Marriages, if taken at the time of registration, are 2s. 7d. (including 1d. for the stamp); but if taken at any time afterwards, an additional fee of 1/- is chargeable for a search extending over a period of not more than the year and 6d. additional or every additional year.

This Certificate being signed and certified as a true copy by an officer in whose custody the original is intrusted, is ordinarily admissible in evidence

Marriage certificate of parents Samuel Katz and Betty Nussbaum, June, 1908.

CLOCKWISE: Parents in happier times, 1925; Parents in front of store, 1930; Helen, 1917; Helen at seven years.

CLOCKWISE: Helen in Frankfurt, 1919; on left with cousin, 1919; school class, 1921, front row center.

THE EARLY YEARS
1909 - 1939

Three-year-old Herta Katz was quite the independent young lady, certainly capable of traveling alone to Aunt Franziska's house one street away. The city of Offenbach in 1912 was not yet plagued with traffic, but an occasional streetcar did pass by. It was over these tracks and in front of this vehicle that I stumbled. My terrified screams and the screech of the streetcar summoned my mother and neighbors on the run. The damage was devastating -- two scraped legs and a total but temporary loss of pride.

Offenbach, the city of my birth, lay across the river Main from Frankfurt. One year after the streetcar incident, for reasons still unknown to me, our family was expelled from Offenbach and my parents moved us to Frankfurt, then a part of Prussia. Our expulsion had something to do with the *big secret*, the first of the skeletons in the closet. As World War I began, the basis of the *secret* became a little clearer.

My father had arrived in Frankfurt in 1890, at the age of nine, having emigrated from Lithuania, a province of Russia, with his parents and sisters. Jews left western Russia by the hundreds of thousands from 1880 until World War I, to escape both the pogroms and the 25 years of mandatory military service required under the Czar. Most went to the United States, but my father's family preferred Germany.

My maternal ancestors had lived in southern Germany for many centuries, always in very small villages. They were not wealthy but they were blessed with many children. With few Jewish families in those villages, it was difficult for young Jews to find compatible marriage partners. So, following an older sister, my mother left for Frankfurt.

Father courted mother with unbelievable persistence for five years. Because German Jews then considered themselves superior to Eastern Jews, Mother saw in a marriage to my father, a social comedown. But, apparently no competition offered her more love and devotion, for she ultimately yielded to his suit.

Thereupon began the difficulties. Not only was Father unable to reside in Frankfurt, he could not enter into a civil marriage, the only recognized legal marriage at the time. To be wed by a rabbi was legally unacceptable. In England, however, aliens could enter into a civil marriage after three days residence. Although it was unheard of in those days for an unmarried couple to travel together, Mother and Father set out for London. In later years, Mother related how humiliated she had felt, making this unchaperoned trip to London before being truly married, always stressing that she returned from London with her virginity intact. The civil marriage was performed, and upon their return to Frankfurt, they were wed in proper religious ceremony.

They settled in Offenbach and promptly, after nine months, I was born. Following our expulsion from Offenbach, we moved to Frankfurt in 1913, when I was four years old. World War I started in August of the following year.

Through marriage, my mother became a Russian subject, and we became enemy aliens, subject to internment. (German law stated that all offspring of aliens assumed the nationality of the father.) Also under German law, all residents, subject or alien, were required to register their residence or change in residence with the local police. By failing to do so, we escaped internment, beginning four years of illegal life. At five years old, however, I was hardly aware of our precarious situation. Fortunately, my uncle owned a four-apartment building. We shared a small apartment with my grandparents, because landlords were obligated to notify the police of any change in their tenants. The building had two stores at street level and was located in the business center of Frankfurt. With my aunt and uncle living just below us, I felt happy and secure, and my two cousins were good company. As I roamed the streets making friends, I hardly recognized the serious problems that faced us, such as the lack of income. Fortunately my uncle, a kind and warm person, was always ready to help.

At six I was to start school but no public school could accept me because of our illegal life. Frankfurt did have, however, a large, progressive school, the *Philanthropin*, founded by the

large secular and religiously liberal part of the Jewish community. It offered four years of elementary, six years of secondary,
and three years of preparatory education necessary for entry
into a university after 1925. The principal graciously accepted
me, despite possible legal consequences. At one point during my
four years of elementary education, I had diphtheria, which
could not be reported to the local health authorities, nor could I
tell any of my friends about this frightful illness. As the
problems with my throat and respiration increased, it became
quite a challenge to keep my secret hidden!

I was a curious, impatient child, and every report card
demanded that my behavior improve. I was eager to learn, but
failed languages regularly. My English language teacher assured
me that I could never master another language; the French
teacher concurred. But years later, when I left Germany for
Holland, I overcame the difficulties of Dutch, and quickly
became fluent in reading, writing and speaking the language.
Fortunately, the same happened with English when I came to
the United States, for I had to start work the next day!

Our history teacher, Professor Hermann Freudenberger,
thoroughly a social democrat, was largely responsible for the
development of my political and social philosophies. The Social
Democrats advocated public ownership of business enterprises
when they felt that private ownership did not serve the public
interest, somewhat akin to the Democratic party in the United
States. A cornerstone of the Social Democratic party was the
preservation of peace; accordingly it supported few appropria-
tions for the military. Through Professor Freudenberger I
experienced the feelings of the German soldiers in November
1918, when they revolted against fighting a losing war. I learned
from him the important difference in being governed by royalty
vs. elected leaders.

At Monmouth College in New Jersey, in 1986, I was asked,

> *"When did you become really aware of the extreme
> polarization between the Left and the Right?"*

Since my first years of historical studies in
school, I have been familiar with those extreme
poles. The implementations changed over the

years; wars were won and lost on both sides, but
it never solved the basic problem. Nobody was
willing to try to find a common ground of
understanding and trust.

There were no bridges possible in Hitler's
Germany. Those on the "wrong" side had to be
removed in any way thinkable, so the "right" side
could flourish and Hitler's "Heaven on Earth"
could be built in Germany!

War's end meant an end to our hiding. A new era had begun,
and we were truly free after four long years. Perhaps now, my
father could support the family, something he had done with
little success during the war years, except for his dealings in the
black market. The skeleton of illegality was gone from our
closet; but a new and more ominous one was forming, created
partially by my mother's prejudices against becoming a Lithuanian citizen.

Lithuania, the formerly Russian territory where my father
was born, became an independent state after the war. My father
had the choice of becoming a Lithuanian or remaining a
Russian citizen. Since German citizenship was practically unat-
tainable, and my mother could not overcome her strong dislike
of being a citizen of any country east of Germany, they decided
to do nothing. Thus we became stateless, the worst and most
dangerous situation. Since my parents harbored no thoughts of
leaving Germany, they did not realize that no country would
accept a person without a legal passport from another country.
(The United States remains one of the few countries which
sometimes makes exceptions; and since World War II, West
Germany can be added to this small list.)

Though stateless, we lived in Frankfurt, free. I went to
school, my father opened a special tobacco shop in an elegant
shopping area, and in 1920 my brother Fred was born. Now
there was sibling competition; I felt hurt and neglected. My
birthday, five days after his arrival, was overlooked!

Though I was told frequently not to get too friendly with
Eastern European children in school, I now needed companion-
ship outside the family, and those girls seemed highly interesting. I learned to lie when visiting their homes and I had to

invent stories as to why they could never come to my house. I
was *never* to tell anybody that we were not German citizens.
Although I did not understand my mother's reasoning, our
terrible secret was constantly on my mind. When my cousin
entered my class, I was warned never to reveal that she was
related to me. (This was no hardship because I considered Anna
stupid and didn't care for her.)

The inflation of 1922-1923 changed many lives. The mark
devalued so fast that most working people had to get paid twice
a day to purchase necessities immediately. My father would
come home in the evening carrying a large suitcase filled with
bills. So ignorant were we of the situation, that we considered
ourselves rich, when in fact we got poorer by the day. In 1925 we
moved out of the small apartment we had shared with my
grandparents, both of whom had died during the war. Our
elegant new home was in a beautiful neighborhood, but I still
had to share a room with my five-year-old brother. His care,
however, was taken over by a hired woman, and we also
acquired a full-time, trained maid. Our family often lived far
beyond its means, for my father was always too willing to fulfill
my mother's expensive desires, assuring her that we could afford
this life style.

Our illusions of wealth brought temporary laughter and
happy times to the family. My parents went to masked balls and
elegant affairs, and even arranged a dance party with a live
orchestra for my friends in our apartment. I was 16, a happy
teenager like my girl friends, with one exception: I went on to
the University at 18, something my mother never understood or
supported. Having known only financial hardship, she wanted to
see me marry as early as possible. My future husband must meet
two conditions -- he must be German-Jewish and RICH. During
a 1925 summer vacation to the seashore, she met her idea of the
perfect man for me. He was 32 years old; I was 16 and
absolutely *not* interested in this "old" man, so I behaved in an
obnoxious manner. I did not want to get married then, or later. I
wanted to study and maybe to teach. I wanted to spend the
evenings with political youth groups. We enjoyed debates,
reading classical and modern plays, and aggravating our parents
by wearing unbecoming and unattractive clothing. Theater and

opera performances, and fashionable horse races were my joy. I also loved the teatime dances at the elegant hotels. Contemporary German literature was a great support.

In a spring, 1983 lecture at Tuft's University, a young woman commented,

> *"I have a completely different view of the times of the Weimar Republic, the '20s in Germany. I thought it was a restless and decadent period and the government too weak to handle the many problems. Why do we know so little about those interesting and lively times you talk about?"*

> I told her, that it had been a restless time, that the German people had suffered greatly after the war, with high unemployment and enormous reparations to the Allies. Then Hitler came to power and began military preparations, defense work and building of the Autobahn, gaining more and more political followers. The aggressive propaganda from the fascist side moved the people to bloody encounters. In retrospect, it seems that Hitler's threats, words and screamings have come to typify the period more than the cultural masterpieces of the day.

Shortly, my father's finances became a fiasco. We moved to less expensive quarters and I began working, something quite unknown in our assumed social circles. We still had a full-time maid and at last, I had my own room. I still attended the theater and opera, albeit in the standing room section, I enjoyed it just as much.

Under the Weimar government, democracy was taken literally, assuring the rights and liberties of everyone. In the middle and late '20's, my friends and I actively supported the junior branches of the Social Democratic party. On our hikes and picnics through the beautiful forests around Frankfurt, our ideological discussions often developed into heated arguments. In our opinion, many social and economic imperfections including poverty could be traced to the timidity of our government. This, we thought, could be remedied by placing

more Social Democrats in the Reichstag. We viewed the Nazis
as a small dark cloud on a far horizon. President Hindenburg
left much to be desired, but we considered him harmless.
National Socialist party members -- Nazis -- were at the
opposite end of the political spectrum from the Social Democrats. Nazis believed that war was a noble activity; that only
fools, cowards and traitors sought peace. Equality had no place
in their philosophy, except among so-called Aryans. There could
be no limit, in their view, on public expenditure for the military.
Unlike the Social Democrats' principle of free elections, the
Nazis believed that all state decisions should be made by the
Fuehrer.

I was now working for Willy Frey, the only honest-to-
goodness Nazi with whom I ever had close contact and I saw a
great challenge developing. I learned a lot from him; he taught
me disciplined and systematic working habits, which I admired,
but otherwise I disliked him intensely. In his late twenties,
married with children, he had already made his fortune out of
nothing. Although Jews comprised about ten percent of
Frankfurt's population, I was the first Jew he had met. Curious
about our different worlds, we at first respected each other's
opinions and worked very well together. Then Willy Frey
became a fanatic follower of Hitler.

At Illinois Central College in 1985, I was asked,

> *"Did any of your friends or acquaintances see any
> good in the Nazi program?*

> Definitely not. I could not be friendly with
> any people whose philosophy was so far removed
> from mine. Those two worlds could never meet.

If Willy Frey hadn't already disliked Jews, I could have given
him reasons to do so. Throughout my apprenticeship, he taught
and I learned his method of earning money so well that I
subsequently started my own business. It was a mail order
business selling liquid soaps, liquid disinfectants and similar
chemical products direct to consumers in minimum 10-liter
containers. My knowledge of this business was adequate, but I
needed a partner who could finance this undertaking. This I

found in a close friend and her husband, who were willing to gamble for a chance to share the profits equally.

We gave the company credibility by buying the name of a man with a doctorate in chemistry. The man was jobless, as were many at that time. It was under these circumstances that DR. PAUL LEHMANN LTD. was born. We established contact with a chemical factory in Hannover which filled our warehouse with cannisters of different sizes of their products, to which we reassigned our own names. A small office with one young secretary and we were ready.

Unemployment was extremely high. We had ads in many major Sunday papers across the country, searching for salesmen to visit small factories, dentists, physicians and larger offices. We promised to pay a 30 percent commission one week after receiving the signed sales order. A salesman had the opportunity to be in charge of his territory if sales warranted. Letters to this effect and mini samples of the merchandise went to every applicant. Given the political situation of the early 1930s, every man needed money. A very few of the thousands of applicants were able to make a living this way. We met with those salespeople and developed good relationships. But the bulk of our income came from the masses of unemployed men, who produced some small orders before deciding that selling looked easier than it was and quit. These orders did add up, since our expenses were minimal. When my partner and his wife left Frankfurt for Paris early in 1933, I bought his share.

When DR. PAUL LEHMANN was about three to four months old, Mr. Frey discovered who was behind the name. I understood why his letters were not the friendliest, and would have felt like a traitor were the man not such an obvious Fascist and chauvinist; but Mr. Frey's wildest threats fell on deaf ears, for I had stolen from him only the ideas in my head.

By the time I was 20, my business was going well. Because of the financial help I could now extend to my parents, my enthusiasm for school waned, but I still attended. I could afford to travel and meet people, which was very important since I had just been jilted by my first serious love. In the summer of 1932 I took a recovery trip to the fashionable and popular island of Norderney, one of the German Frisian Islands in the North Sea.

It was quite proper for a young girl to go alone to dances, especially to dance-teas in the afternoon. The second afternoon I was attending a dance on the beach, enjoying iced coffee, the warm breeze and the good orchestra, when a young man came all the way across the dance floor to my table. He looked no more than 18, and being 23, I was reluctant to dance with him, but I loved dancing too much to resist. It evolved that we were both from Frankfurt and that he was 28. Although I would have preferred a better dancer, I had few offers this day. During my three-week stay, I met many interesting men, but Siegfried Wohlfarth was the most persistent. In fact, he fell in love much too fast for me. Siegfried came from an orthodox, patrician German-Jewish family. Our religious beliefs and political opinions were identical. He was very well educated, intelligent and quite serious, a CPA who never made major decisions lightly. He surprised even himself by asking to marry me after only 10 days. I had to refuse. I liked him and admired his understanding of fields practically unknown to me; but I let him know that my feelings did not match his. He waited patiently, and early in January 1933, I agreed to marry him.

On January 30, 1933, President Hindenburg involuntarily appointed Adolf Hitler chancellor of Germany. Before this, his name for Hitler had been a contemptuous *Der Bayerische Korporal!* Everybody knew that Hitler's government was anti-Semitic. There was despair in Jewish circles. We followed the complete and frightening legal changes which affected nearly everyone. The Communists and the Social Democrats could not build a combined front against the common enemy, and even fought each other. All hope for the destruction of the dictatorship was lost after the Reichstag fire early in March 1933. Political aggression, insecurity and fear led to many suicides. But nobody could possibly conceive of what was about to happen. There had been pogroms against the Jews and genocides against a variety of peoples in centuries past, but organized mass-murder in this progressive century seemed preposterous. Many people, my parents included, tried to wait it out -- it is so difficult to leave your home for an unknown country. It seemed that it *couldn't* be long, before it all would be over.

Before we had made definite marriage plans, Siegfried, under the new regime, lost his job as a bankruptcy officer of the courts. After three-and-a-half years, I had to quit my university studies, as there were now no Jewish teachers. Against the advice of Siegfried's parents, who could not understand that people without income do get married, we continued our plans. They were not too happy with his choice, because of my father's Lithuanian background. The Wohlfarth family was quite orthodox (Siegfried's maternal grandfather had been a rabbi), while my family was less orthodox and I was a hopeless liberal. Siegfried's mother subsequently announced to her 29-year-old son that she would not give her permission to the marriage, which upset us very much. Convinced that I would impress his parents if we talked in person, he arranged a meeting. I remember every word of this visit, despite fifty years and so many monumental changes. Siegfried had designed new furniture for his room which he wanted me to see, and on that pretense I was invited to the family home one evening. Siegfried's mother served tea and confections, he left the room, and she and I were alone. Tall as her son, slender and serious, Mrs. Wohlfarth was probably just as uncomfortable as I. She reiterated that she could not give her permission to such an unwise decision, despite the fact that I had my own business and could support us adequately. You see, a woman's being the primary bread-winner was unheard of in those days. We both were very polite, albeit somewhat cool. She remained firm in her decision, but I reminded her softly, "I am very sorry that you cannot agree with the two of us, but you should consider one fact: whether you want it or not, I will carry your name, Mrs. Wohlfarth, until the end of my life." As it happened, this was not to be.

As my parents had done, we planned two marriage ceremonies. We wanted to leave Germany as soon as possible, but I was stateless and no other country would consider me. A civil marriage ceremony to a German citizen in the Roemerberg, the century-old city hall of Frankfurt, would, however, make me a German citizen automatically. Immediately following the ceremony, we left for France, where we had some connections and hoped to move to avoid the increasingly harsh restrictions under

DER·ANKE

Left, building where Helen lived with her family until leaving for Holland. Below, same building after air attacks.

(While the quality of many war period photos is not the best, considering the restrictions and massive loss of property, we are fortunate to have them at all.)

CLOCKWISE: Wedding day, June, 1933; with Siegfried at Scheveningen, Netherlands, 1935; Doris, 1939; mother and daughter in Amsterdam -- October 4, 1939; parents and child, 1938.

the new regime, but it proved impossible.

Returning to Frankfurt, we wanted to complete the marriage ritual, and thus went through a religious ceremony. The same rabbi that had married our parents, married us. My parents hosted a small dinner party, and although Siegfried's parents attended the ceremony, they were not invited to the meal. Said my father, "Who does not want my daughter, for whatever reason, does not have to eat my food!"

Conditions for the Jews of Germany were declining steadily. Jewish businesses and therefore Jewish income, began to suffer gravely. Siegfried developed a plan, complicated but feasible. An old friend, A.G., who was just starting his own metal business, wanted Siegfried to help him with financial and legal advice. Since A.G. was also Jewish, he planned to go into business in Holland, Belgium or Great Britain. Holland was interested in having this German company open a metal-nickel-melting factory, as it would provide jobs for Dutch workers. The state agreed to issue working permits for aliens who were needed to run the complete plant. A.G., his brother and sister and Siegfried received working permits and we moved to Amsterdam in June, 1934.

At the University of Rochester (New York) in 1984, I was asked:

> *"Why did so many German Jews commit suicide or wait until it was too late and then were deported to Poland and killed?"*

> I explained that nobody could foresee the actual plans of the German government. Even the people who took Hitler's book *Mein Kampf* seriously and did want to leave, found it unbelievably difficult to enter another country. It wasn't Germany that prevented the Jews from leaving; the problem was finding countries to accept them. Germany did prohibit emigrants from taking money or valuables, and every minute of packing was closely observed by German guards. Businesses, real estate or farms practically had to be given away.

March 10, 1933 -- thousands and thousands of books by the finest and best-known writers, scientists, artists, poets were, under order of the new government, burned. In every city, books were carried out of the libraries, and universities, to be added to the infernos. Students and professors of the new regime were proud to destroy the best Germany had ever created. This was not the first time that books had been burned in Germany. In 1817 in the old Wartburg where the troubadours met and competed, the Wartburg of Martin Luther witnessed a book burning where everything that was non-conformist, including Voltaire, was destroyed. Heinrich Heine, a victim of this event, then spoke those prophetic words, "This is just the prelude; where books are being burned, the next fire will be for human beings."

Leaving Frankfurt was made very difficult by the authorities, who wanted to be rid of the Jews, but demanded that we first complete an incredible amount of paperwork. There were reports about our legal standing, records from the tax offices, bank records and endless lists of furniture, clothing, kitchen utensils and household goods. All of our 450 books had to be listed. When the moving days finally came, one or two watchmen constantly monitored what went into the large wooden boxes, and another person went through every book. This was nerve-wracking, but not as devastating as saying goodbye to our parents, my 14-year-old brother, Siegfried's younger brother, and all our friends from childhood.

I sold my mail order business, our only income. With that money and our meager savings, we would be able to buy household items before leaving for Amsterdam. That I did not know how to keep house or even to cook, was quite unimportant. Since we could take only 250 mark out of the country, we decided to spend our money before leaving, and bought such luxury items as a small electric refrigerator, a vacuum cleaner, an electric floor polisher, which certainly were above our financial means.

At a small Eastern college I was once asked,

> _"How did the German authorities know who was_
> _Jewish, so long before it was mandatory for every_

Jew to wear the yellow star?"

In Germany as in many other European
countries, there is never a collection after services at churches or synagogues. An orthodox
Jew cannot carry or touch money on Saturdays
or high holidays. Therefore, every taxpayer has
to declare to which religious group he belongs
and pay a "church tax," which then is divided
among the main religious communities. Jewish
citizens were, naturally, on lists separate from
the rest of the population.

In Holland, after the invasion in 1940, it was
quite easy for the Germans to get nearly complete lists of Jews, for there was only one Jewish
community, and every Jew attending religious
services was a member. The police department
also maintained a complete list of all refugees.
Those were made available on request for the
German invaders and for the Jewish Council, an
organization created by the Germans.

Strangely enough, the Portuguese Jewish
community, which dated back almost 400 years
from the time of the Inquisition in Spain and
Portugal, was presumed by the Germans to
belong to the Portuguese. Portugal was neutral,
so it was assumed that those members could not
be deported. Near the end of the war, the
German occupying forces discovered that those
Portuguese Jews had lived for generations in
Holland, and were Dutch citizens of Portuguese
descent. A very large part of this community was
summarily deported and destroyed.

We moved to a small, modern apartment in Amsterdam,
comfortable and quite inexpensive. I could not get a working
permit and since Siegfried's job paid poorly in the beginning, we
lived quite modestly.

Both of us were eager to learn the culture of our new home,
but there was a great difference in the way we adjusted to the
changes in our lives. Siegfried had a deep love for Germany and
never overcame his resentment that this new right-wing Fascist

government had changed everything and everybody. Formerly a free-lance music critic in his leisure time, Siegfried decided that he could not listen to another concert until this horrid nightmare was over. His life was cut short beforehand.

In contrast, I felt no roots. My education, my formative years had the European stamp, and I still love to visit Germany, but where is home? Probably nowhere. My happiest and my saddest years were in Holland, but it was not truly home.

Our housing development filled with more young couples, some also from Germany, with similar adjustment problems, which made life a little more enjoyable. Siegfried's income increased, so we could afford a telephone and a modest social life. Our parents, old friends and other close relatives occasionally were given permission to leave Germany for a short visit.

In 1936 I learned that two brothers, Ernst and Otto, with whom I had been acquainted in Frankfurt were living in Amsterdam. I had known Ernst fairly well, but Otto only casually. Siegfried and I became friendly with Otto and his friend Ilse, who had also followed him to Amsterdam. Otto had arrived in Holland shortly before Hitler came to power, for he had begun to feel insecure in Germany. Otto's parents, although quite wealthy, did not consider education a necessity, and Otto lived with them in a beautiful apartment. He was interested in economics, financial affairs, political trends, and there was no doubt in his mind that Hitler would be powerful. His beliefs influenced his family to leave Germany while there was still time to bring their wealth.

Otto, always a loner and usually in disagreement with his brother, had few friends and showed little interest in other people. So it was to the surprise of his parents that he brought with him to Amsterdam a woman friend whose background was absolutely foreign to them. Ilse was the only daughter of a well-known Frankfurt banker, attractive and petite, well-educated and sophisticated, bubbly and outgoing. She had been raised like a true princess and had fallen in love with Otto. Ilse had very little money and refused any from her father, who objected to her adventure; nor would she take any from Otto. When I met her, she lived in a blue collar neighborhood in Amsterdam, had a small furnished room and used her talent as a dressmaker in this part of town. This unusual couple brought some important changes into our life, not immediately, but slowly, as our relationship developed.

Early in 1936, when we had been in Holland about two years, I developed nightly anxiety attacks, which were quite frightening. A medical examination showed no physical changes, but a few weeks later I began fearing heights. The fears became stronger just by imagining a high point in any building. I was convinced that I was losing my mind and did not talk about my experiences to the physician or even to Siegfried. My complete daily life was consumed with fighting those frightening imaginations. I touched no books, took no walks; acrophobia was overcoming me.

I began pondering how to carry this heavy mental burden in a way that nobody, including Siegfried, would notice. I forced myself to go to higher floors in department stores and look from the inside to the street. The true fear was that I felt such a magnetic pull from the ground, a feeling that there was no other way but to jump out the window.

One day an acquaintance called to invite me to her home for tea. She lived on the fourth floor of a large apartment building. If I wanted to get better, I decided, I must through this visit to prove to myself that I could do it. The fear, the anxiety and the pounding of my heart were greater than I had ever experienced. I gripped the armrest of my chair so tightly during my visit that my knuckles were white. But I made it! This was the slow beginning of a very difficult period of overcoming my phobia.

By this time, it was impossible to take more than 10 marks out of Germany. Siegfried's parents, who had some unreported savings, began to feel uneasy about this. We were advised by a reliable source that there was a way to smuggle money out of Germany, but it had to be brought personally to Cologne. I was selected to go to Frankfurt in the summer of 1936 to collect this money and bring it to Cologne. When the money arrived in Holland, which nobody could guarantee, 30 percent would be deducted as a fee. The additional temptation to visit the family was great.

My parents were, naturally, anxiously awaiting my visit, but

the tension of this trip increased my acrophobia, and I had to
tell them that I could not stay with them, for they lived in a fifth-
floor apartment walk-up. I was numb, thinking about the stairs,
because on each landing was a seat with a long window facing
the street. In my parents' dining room was a balcony door,
leading to an unusual three-cornered veranda. There seemed to
be only one solution -- my in-laws lived in a first-floor
apartment, but how could I stay there and not hurt my parents'
feelings? I had to tell them of my strange affliction without
letting anyone else know.

They handled my confession lovingly. I stayed with
Siegfried's parents, who were very happy and never asked any
questions. But I had, for my own satisfaction, to go to my
parents' apartment. When I arrived, my father had the door to
the veranda nailed closed, so that nobody could go out there
during my visit. He made endless trips up and down the stairs
with me and in the end, I felt quite victorious.

Everything went well, although it was indeed frightening to
enter Germany after two years and face the Nazis on the
border. I left Frankfurt for Cologne by train, carrying the money
in my pocketbook, and was greatly surprised that the people
who met me on the train were relatives of a good friend of mine.
They were reliable and hospitable, and at the end of three tense
weeks, our money did arrive. After this adventure into Nazi
territory, it was exciting to leave Germany and enter peaceful,
beautiful Holland.

This period, 1936, was the time of Civil War in Spain. With
no censorship in Holland, we were completely aware of this war,
so generously supported by Fascist Germany and Italy, and
ultimately involving the Soviet Union and many other countries.
It soon became apparent that this Civil War was a general
rehearsal for World War II. The German bombing of Guernica,
the most important city in northern Spain in April of 1937, was a
prelude to the terrors of war that would be with us for years to
come. Franco insisted that the people of Guernica had destroyed their own town, and Hitler ordered that an international
investigation of Guernica be rejected under all circumstances.

Otto was upset about those events, just as he had been
concerned and indignant about Italy's invasion of Ethiopia in

1935. He may then have been making plans to leave Europe, but
he did not talk much about it, especially since Ilse was
considering changing her business from dressmaking into something more elegant. She planned to rent a place in a fashionable
neighborhood where she could live, work, and at the same time
receive her clients. But when she discussed her plans, she always
ended by saying she hoped to find somebody who would draw
up plans, find the right place, and furnish it completely for her.
Was she a princess or not? Money, she assured us, would not be
a problem. She merely wanted her new home to be furnished
right down to the matches for the gas stove. It must be so
exquisite that her clients would say, "Oh, how unusual and
beautiful; who did this?"

Early in 1937 we learned that we could expect a baby in
October. While we were extremely happy, our income damp-
ened our outlook for the future. Siegfried could not get a raise,
and it was impossible for me to get a working permit. Suddenly
it occurred to me that *I* could fulfill Ilse's great wish, although I
was well aware of my limited knowledge in this field of interior
design. I would be involved in purchasing and contracting work,
creating the atmosphere Ilse expected in her new surroundings.
But it would serve her purpose and mine, for I was hoping that,
if successful, I could start a career to help our financial situation.

Ilse seemed as enthusiastic as I. I made it clear to her that I
did not want any fee or payment; I only hoped that she would be
out of town while I made my arrangements. That was exactly
what she had wanted. I told her that I hoped that through her
clients, I could build an interesting and profitable enterprise.

While she and Otto went on an extensive vacation, I found
an apartment that offered all the necessities. Leaving me with a
large amount of money, she agreed to call weekly so I could
inform her of my progress, and when they might return.
Siegfried had a talent for furniture design, which we combined
with my taste for arrangement and color, and geared to Ilse's
personality, a simple Bauhaus style with bold lines and colors.
She had two large rooms with kitchen and bath in an older
building with high ceilings. The back room was her workroom,
divided by unusual screens to form a private dressing room with
large mirrors. In front were a fireplace and three high windows

Brochure advertising (Helen) Herta Wohlfarth's home interiors business.

to the street. Draperies and upholstered furniture were silver, the floor covering a bright red. The other furniture was ebony, built into the wall. The bed folded into the wall, making way for a table and three dining room chairs, black with the same silvery material as the easy chairs and the corner couch. Still, the room was in no way crowded. I hired a full-time maid for her, purchased the linens and kitchen gear, and I told her that even the matches were now ready on the stove! It was exciting to see their faces when they returned, overcome by the beauty and utility of her new home/office.

It was on this project that I met Ab Reusink, a contractor, carpenter and a creative wizard who made the built-in furniture. Ab was always ready to give me advise, which I greatly needed four years later in 1941, when events became life or death matters. Ab was always the first to offer support or help, and was a selfless friend to us long after the war.

Ilse developed a satisfied clientele, and with her reception room as an example of my work, I gained many customers. I often helped newcomers, from Germany and elsewhere, find affordable apartments in the right vicinity and advised them on how to adapt their belongings to the Dutch living quarters. I had connections with artisans, mechanics and craftsmen which made newcomers' adjustments to a strange country and language somewhat easier.

Our wish for a child was fulfilled on October 28, 1937, when our daughter Doris was born. My childhood friend Gerda from Frankfurt, a beautiful, blue-eyed blonde, had moved to Amsterdam with her parents in the early 20's. I introduced Gerda to Juro, a bachelor friend I had met in Norderney in 1932, and they were married in 1936. Their daughter Vera was the first of the four girls born to our close circle of friends in 1937.

My closest friend Irene, whose husband was Siegfried's colleague, lived across the street. Their daughter Margrit, the surviving premature twin, was born two months after Doris. Early in 1940, they moved to a house near the North Sea. Eva and Walter, our next door neighbors, had Miriam, the youngest of our four children. Above them lived a couple, Ilse and George, who although they remained childless, found satisfaction in helping each of us. Out of our group of five happy couples and four wanted babies, at the end of the war, only Juro, Doris, Miriam and I were alive.

Most Jews in Germany were without income, professionals and storekeepers alike. Forced sale of Jewish properties had put millions of marks into the government's hands. What would happen next? Decree after decree was beginning to limit the chances of survival for the Jews in Germany. Newspapers printed articles like:

WHAT TO DO WITH JEWS?
and
JEWS FOR SALE -- WHO WANTS THEM? -- NO ONE!

Switzerland decided not only to refuse large numbers of Jewish refugees, (which meant their return to Germany) but suggested that Germany mark Jews' passports with a red "J" one inch high. Other countries made similar decisions.

On October 31, 1938, the Polish government revoked the passports of citizens who had lived out of the country for more than five years, unless a special visa had been issued. For the Polish Jews there were no special visas, and Germany inherited 15,000 stateless Jews. The Gestapo immediately deported them to the Polish border, without informing the Polish government of its action. They herded men, women and children into railroad cars going east, to a country that would not accept them. Most of the refugees spent the winter in primitive camps in a no-man's land between the two countries.

Herschel Grynszpan, a young Polish Jew living in Paris, got news that his family, German residents since 1911, had been deported to Zbonszyn without notice. They were broke and desperate. Four days after receiving this message, 17-year-old Herschel walked into the German embassy in Paris, was received by Third Secretary Ernst vom Rath, pulled out a gun and shot him.

Germany made full use of the attack after vom Rath died. All Jewish newspapers and magazines were stifled, and on November 9, 1938, a series of massive anti-Semitic demonstrations began throughout the country. After being arrested, Grynszpan was transferred from prison to prison. Apparently the Germans wanted to prove that this attack was a conspiracy of Jews world-wide, and they intended to hold Grynszpan as a pawn for eventual exchange. One billion marks was the punitive levy assessed on Jewish property to be paid by the German Jews in quarterly installments of five percent for the murder of vom Rath. The fourth installment, due on November 10, 1939, was raised to ten percent, when the total Jewish property in Germany was calculated at five billion marks. After the shooting in November, Grynszpan was jailed by the French, who scheduled a trial. But the plaintiffs, members of vom Rath's family, were Germans, and therefore could not be admitted to France.

Before Grynszpan's future could be resolved, the Germans swarmed south in all directions to capture Paris, in June of 1940. The French police at the Sante prison abandoned a convoy of prisoners which included Grynszpan. He might have been at liberty had he not knocked on prison doors across France and pursued the French police to take him back into custody. The Germans traced him to the Toulouse prison and quickly seized him. Grynszpan's first trial was in May of 1942, after which his family claimed he had been executed. Others maintain that he survived and assumed another identity after the war.

About this time, our friends Ilse and Otto decided they could wait no longer to leave Europe. They left the exquisite apartment, and it became my problem to convert all their belongings into cash. They went first to England where they decided, after all those years, to get married. It was much easier for married couples to acquire the necessary permits, visas or living quarters. From England they went to Havana, Cuba, to await a visa for the United States. I saw Ilse and Otto last in 1947, when Doris and I arrived in New York. They seemed to be enjoying life, and we corresponded until my last letter was not answered.

Siegfried's mother's family, long-time residents of England, visited Amsterdam frequently. His first cousin, Stanley Lissack, arrived at our house in Amsterdam for dinner on the evening of November 9, a day of infamy for every German-Jewish family. Late that evening, a barrage of unprecedented ferocity began all over Germany. Officially it was impromptu, but in every town the events were identical. Jewish men were harassed

Synagogue at Frankfurt's Boerne Platz, in the early 20th century. Below, the same synagogue in flames on November 9, 1938.

unbelievably and taken to concentration camps. Synagogues in small towns and large cities alike were burned to the ground, while police watched.

My hometown of Frankfurt, with its 35,000 Jews, had four synagogues.The pogrom started with the burning of the synagogues and all their sacred contents. Jewish stores were destroyed and the windows shattered. It was truly *Kristallnacht*, "the night of broken glass."

Nearly every house was searched for Jewish men. The SA, in plain clothes, came to my parents' apartment to arrest my father and 18-year-old brother, after a "helpful" neighbor showed them where in the roomy attic those Jews could be hiding. My brother was deported to Buchenwald, as was my brother-in-law Hans.

The German camps such as Buchenwald, Dachau, and Bergen-Belsen, were concentration camps where thousands and thousands of people died for a variety of reasons. The six *extermination* camps, started in 1940 and fully operative by late 1941, were located in Poland.

Until the war began, it was possible to get people out of a concentration camp with a valid visa for immigration to another country. When my father had been arrested earlier in the summer of 1938, we obtained permission from the Dutch authorities for him to come to Holland. He was released from the camp, but did not want to leave Germany without his wife and son. Despite the loss of his business, he was still stubbornly optimistic about the future of the Jews in Germany. When he was arrested later on *Kristallnacht*, the SA man -- seeing the visa to Holland attached to his passport -- said, "You idiot, what are you still doing here? Tomorrow morning I will meet you at the train station to see that you go to Amsterdam."

The phone call that Father was coming to Amsterdam was our first news of this horrifying night. Stanley offered to help Siegfried's brother and his wife and my brother get to England. We next arranged for my mother and Siegfried's parents to come to Holland. By early 1939, our entire family had made arrangements to leave Germany.

Ena and Sidney, cousins of Siegfried, took my brother Fred into their home in London, although they had never met him before. They had two young children, and Ena worked day and night as a volunteer, caring for refugee children. But Fred was homesick, lonely for his friends, and one day he was contacted by a girl he had known from Frankfurt. She was working in a children's home and they tried to arrange a meeting. Whether the girl told Fred of the outbreak of diphtheria at the home and the necessary quarantine, and he decided to ignore it, or whether she failed to mention it, is lost to memory; but she did come to visit. When Ena heard of the disease, she was understandably very upset. Now her children could not go to school, Stanley had to stay home from work, and Fred had to take different quarters. There were refugee camps around London, and there Fred waited until his visa for the United States arrived.

Fortunately this event did not hurt the friendly feelings in the family. After the war, Ena visited us in Amsterdam, and Robert and I were later guests at their country home in Essex. Fred and his family kept in contact, and Ena and I still correspond.

Following our lecture in the local synagogue at Palm Springs in 1983, someone asked,

> *"Didn't many countries, especially the United States, admit political refugees freely?"*

> If this had been true, many of the Jews and other "enemies of the Third Reich" would have left Germany at once, and the death toll would have been substantially less. Many German Jews illegally crossed the "green borders" into France, Belgium or Holland, but nearly all were caught in the German invasion of May, 1940. Great Britain also did very little to aid refugees in entering that country, except for their children's transports, a service the United States categorically denied. The British also allowed single women with working permits to enter as domestics. The misconception that the United States maintained an open-door policy toward Jewish refugees is destroyed in several recent books, among them Arthur D. Morse's *While Six Million Died* and Walter Laqueur's *The Terrible Secret*.

But the research of David S. Wyman, published under the title *The Abandonment of the Jews: America and the Holocaust 1941-1945*, is the definitive revelation of America's shocking quota system.

Juro's wife, Gerda, and daughter, Vera, prior to 1942.

Juro in 1945.

PART II:
1939 - 1945

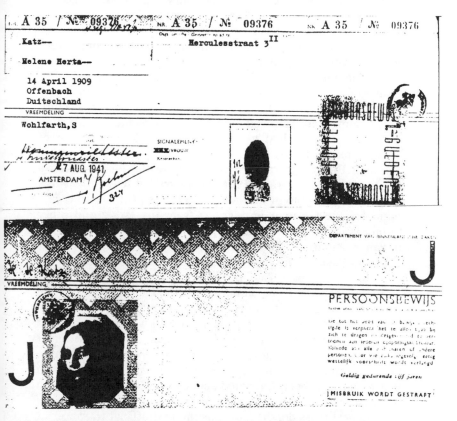

Identification card, 1941, the two J's indicating Jewish status.

Early in September 1939, the Germans invaded Poland, having annexed Austria in 1938 and occupied Czechoslovakia in early 1939. England declared war on Germany, in support of its agreement with Poland. As the Polish government saw Warsaw bombed into oblivion, it began to accept the reality of Germany's overwhelming military power.

From 1933 until the beginning of the war in September 1939, there had been arrests, building of concentration camps, deportations, executions, tortures, and beating of thousands of German Jews and opponents of the regime. The camps were crowded with nearly as many Gentiles as Jews. Social Democrats, Communists, Free Masons, Jehovah's Witnesses, homosexuals, Catholic priests and Protestant pastors -- in short, everybody who did not march to the same tune as the Third Reich. Some were released after a time, many more were shot, and the ones who had to stay had the backbreaking job of building more camps.

Adolf Eichmann was ordered to make the former Austria and the Bohemia-Moravia Protectorate free of Jews -- *judenrein* -- as fast as possible in the fall of 1939. The plan was to create room for the German immigrants from the Baltic and other former Poles of German ancestry. A Jewish reservation, like the Indian reservations in the United States, was planned near Lublin in Poland. The Jews of Austria and Czechoslovakia were deported in masses to Lublin, which was in no way prepared for an onslaught of this size. Hans Frank, the German chief of the newly named General Government, headquartered in Cracow, which was hardly touched during the war. It was to Cracow that Frank had the golden carriage of the Queen of Holland brought for his use. When the Lublin deportations were reported to him, he went immediately to the Berlin headquarters to complain that he had not been informed about the plans in Poland. The response was nothing more than an apology.

The next mass deportation was the first official transport of

1100 German Jews from Stettin, also to Lublin. The rumor was
that 100,000 or more Jews would be settled there, with Danzig's
12,000 to be next.

The truth was, that Germany had thousands and thousands
of concentration camps, an unknown large number of forced
labor camps -- some of them built into mountains or underground -- and also transit camps. There were transit camps in
every occupied country. Here, Jewish prisoners were shelved
until being shipped by cattle car to the newly created extermination camps in Poland.

The non-citizens of the German-occupied territories were
the first to be deported. By July 1942, the extermination camps
were ready to receive and the trains came, daily and regularly,
containing at least 1000 but often many more Jews, who did not
know where they were going or what to expect. And after the
lists of stateless persons were exhausted, Jewish citizens of the
same countries went the same route, in every one of the
countries occupied by Germany.

I have always been bothered by the claim that nothing was
known of the genocide in Europe until the Allies liberated the
concentration camps at war's end. On September 12, 1939, not
even two weeks into the war, the *New York Times* reported from
Berlin:

> "The first intimation that 'a solution of the
> Jewish problem' in Poland is on the German
> Polish agenda has been revealed in a "special
> report" of the official German News Bureau that
> emanates from Polish territory, now occupied by
> the German military. In view of the world
> refugee problem and the individual suffering
> created in the last six years by the German deter-
> mination to rid their country of Jews, the impli-
> cations of the 'solution of the Jew problem in
> Poland' -- were it carried out on the German
> model -- are ominous."

A few days before the attack on Poland, at a meeting called
by Hitler for his military chiefs, General Halder took the
following notes of Hitler's admonition to his generals:

"If Chamberlain does not put another
Munich on me, we will attack as planned.
Essentially all depends on me, on my existence,
because of my political talents. Furthermore,
probably no one will ever again have the confidence of the whole German people as I have.
Probably no man in the future will have more
authority than I have. My existence is a factor of
great value.... No one knows how long I shall live.
Therefore a showdown had better take place
now; the most iron determination on our part.
No shrinking back from anything. A life and
death struggle.... The destruction of Poland has
priority.... A quick decision, in view of the
season.

"I shall give a propaganda reason for starting
the war. Never mind if it is plausible or not. The
victor will not be asked afterwards whether he
told the truth or not. In starting and waging a
war it is not right that matters, but victory. Close
your hearts to pity! Act brutally! Eighty million
people must obtain what is their right.... Be hard
and remorseless! Be steeled against all signs of
compassion! Whoever has pondered over this
world order knows that its meaning lies in the
success of the best by the means of force."

In a further ludicrous move, the Propaganda Ministry
disclosed late in September 1939, the *Ten Commandments of the
German Soldier*. Four are selected here:

3: A soldier must spare the life of any opponent
   who surrenders.
4: A soldier must treat prisoners humanely.
5: A soldier must respect the Red Cross.
6: A soldier must respect the neutrality of non-
   combating states.

These and thousands of other informative news reports
could be found in the American newspapers before the United
States ever entered the war.

My in-laws lived in a small apartment nearby, but my parents stayed with us, awaiting permission to emigrate to the United States. Ironically, considering my mother's former prejudices, it was my father's birth in Lithuania that saved their lives, because the Lithuanian visa quota had not yet been reached. They arrived in the United States in January 1940, about the same time as Siegfried's brother Hans and his wife Alice. They had been in England with my brother Fred, thanks to the help of cousin Stanley. At this time, every country had a quota of immigrants who could, after obtaining affidavits from sponsors and passing certain health standards, enter and stay in the country. The United States' quota for Germans at that time was 28,000 persons per year, but from 1933 through 1938, less than half of each annual quota was filled. If my parents and my brother had been subject to the German quota rather than the Lithuanian, they never would have seen the United States or the end of the war. The reasons for this inexcusable neglect are documented in many historical reports.

We had planned a house-warming party at Irene's on Saturday, May 11, 1940, when we heard rumors that the Dutch army was mobilizing. Siegfried, the pragmatist, suggested that we all take our children and stay the night, in case something was brewing. The party never happened, for during the early morning hours of May 10, hell broke loose. We were awakened by the roar and flak of hundreds of airplanes. The radio announced the *blitzkrieg* invasion by German paratroopers who had parachuted into the country at 3 a.m. Some friends came over during the night. Together we did not feel so helpless, but we did realize that Holland was powerless to stop this wave that would eventually swallow us all. There were serious discussions of suicide; we knew how desperate our situation was. This move had destroyed all hope of our leaving. Over the radio we heard the order that all German citizens were under house arrest and not allowed on the streets. Not only were we the hunted Jews of Germany; as German citizens, we were now enemies of Holland! That morning, the food stores opened at the regular time, and although our men did not go to work, we women went to the store to get food supplies.

Four-and-a-half days later, Holland capitulated and was occupied by German troops. On the last day of the war, after the heavy bombing of Rotterdam, the rumor spread that a British ship was waiting in the Dutch harbor of Ijmuiden, ready to take anybody wishing to go to England. But how could we get to the seaport? We were not allowed to leave the house and had no means of transportation. Very much against Siegfried's wishes, I walked the streets to find a taxi willing to drive us to Ijmuiden. I found none.

After the war, we learned that some second cousins of Siegfried's had tried to contact us, but the telephone lines were cut. Although the ship was only half filled, it had to leave that afternoon. Siegfried's relatives reached the port and were able to sail to safety in England.

Schiller begins his historical drama *Kabale und Liebe* with the words, *Die schoenen Tage von Aranjuez sie sind vorbei!* Verdi incorporated this story into his opera *Louise Miller*, in which this line is translated, "The beautiful days at Aranjuez, they are gone forever." Those words haunt me still.

Life under the occupation seemed endurable, but when the Germans were victorious in Belgium and France a short time later, depression and hopelessness overcame us. Siegfried, the rational, systematic organizer, always the pessimist, developed his prognosis in September of 1940. He was certain that if the Germans did not attack England next, the delay would cost them the war. He was unclear when this would be or if we would be alive by then, but he made the preparations he considered necessary. One day, he expected, we would be forced to separate from our child. Perhaps he was remembering the German children who were accepted in England by transport a year or two earlier. He wanted three-year-old Doris to have every chance to stay alive, even if it were not possible for us. We had enough family in America, where she would be welcome. To make this separation easier for her, we began to distance ourselves from Doris emotionally -- no hugging, no holding. In retrospect I am not so sure this was right, but who can judge at such moments? By the time the parting actually happened about two years later, we had no tears left. This well-organized preparation certainly saved her life, but those two years may have deadened something in her that never could be awakened.

The next problem was disposal of our belongings. We knew

we could trust Ab Reusink. In 1941, we sold him everything in our apartment, and he paid us -- on paper! Ab came alone every night to remove and hide our books, silver, china, linens, typewriter, clothing and other items. Two years later, months after we had left the apartment with all the furniture and had faithfully paid the monthly rent (what optimists we were), a special department of the occupational forces arrived. Ab protested that those were his belongings and produced the three-year old contract. The Germans had to pay him the amount of the contract, and this money came in very handy for us later. I still have the receipt stating that the Department Rosenberg had cleared out the apartment of the family Wohlfarth.

We wanted a will directing our child's future, but when we suggested that Ab be Doris' guardian, he had to refuse. As a practicing Catholic with three children, he would gladly take Doris into his home, but would be obliged to raise her as Catholic. We did not want Doris brought up in any religion, but wanted to expose her to all choices, so at 18 she could make her own decision. About a year later, we met Rinus Hille, a man who understood our concerns and was happy to take guardianship of Doris, should it become necessary.

Shortly before the invasion of Holland, Siegfried had convinced the owner of the factory that he and his family should utilize their American visas, advice that saved the lives of A.G., his wife and two children, his sister, and her husband. German Jews living outside Germany had lost their citizenship, so Hans, Siegfried's brother who lived in New Jersey, was trying to buy us all visas for Cuba. No plausible avenue of escape was being overlooked.

The non-aggression pact between the Soviet Union and Germany was not even two years old when, on June 22, 1941, Germany invaded Russia. We saw this as a most hopeful event. The invading Germans moved ahead with unbelievable speed, while the Soviets retreated, fighting. The Germans were already talking of victory and being home at Christmas, as they moved deeper and deeper into the Russian Motherland. But like Napoleon, who advanced just as fast and also too far when he invaded Russia on June 22, 1812, the Germans did not consider the early and harsh Russian winter. Following the German army very closely were the *Einsatztruppen*, secret, specially trained *SS* soldiers who, in every occupied town, rounded up the Jews for death by a variety of means.

I am most often asked,
"*Why the Jews?*"

> My answer is that Hitler did not invent anti-Semitism. At this time, less than one percent of the German population was Jewish, yet this blood bath was not enough for many people. They would have endured a longer war if this Jewish problem could have been solved completely. More than three million Polish Jews were killed, and the pitiful remnants who returned from those horrendous experiences were, in many towns, then killed by the residents. Two-thirds of the European Jewry was removed, but it was seemingly not enough. Not only the Jews were eliminated, though. Of the eleven million civilians exterminated, five million were non-Jews. Gypsies, Slavs, homosexuals, Jehovah's Witnesses, Russian prisoners of war and other groups shared the stigma of being unworthy to live.

This was simply one part of the Final Solution, the intricate program to cleanse Europe of the unwanted people. Announced at a meeting of the higher party functionaries on January 20, 1942, at Wannsee (close to Berlin), the plan was unprecedented in history. Never had genocide been worked out in such detail, with such perfect programming and infallible accuracy. The net in Germany and most occupied countries of Europe was so tight that escape was practically impossible.

British reporter Gitta Sereny, author of *Into That Darkness*, helped me better understand the events that began in 1942. She interviewed Franz Stangl, commandant of the extermination camps of Sobibor and Treblinka, during April and June of 1971 while he was being held in the Remand Prison in Duesseldorf, Germany. Stangl, who was awaiting the result of his appeal against a life sentence, died before the decision. Sereny also interviewed every person around the world with whom Stangl had had contact, including his closest relatives.

Stangl told of being promoted from a police officer in Vienna after the Austrian Anschluss of 1938, to work at Hartheim Castle in Austria. He insisted that he did not realize this was the Night and Fog (*Nacht und Nebel*) project, but it was during this period that Hitler signed the decree to begin extermination of the physically and mentally handicapped. Thousands and thousands of mentally or terminally ill people were taken to isolated buildings or castles and disposed of by various experimental methods of so-called "euthanasia."

Early in 1941, the Vatican expressed dissatisfaction with this undertaking, and as a consequence, a change of procedure followed. In addition to the six facilities where those experiments were undertaken, there were 11 "special hospitals" where children were put to sleep by injections. The "patients" stayed only a few hours, and nobody ever got out alive.

The extermination of Germans certified as incurably insane began in December 1939 or January 1940. Hitler gave verbal instructions to his physician to stop euthanasia. However, Dr. Brandt (who was not an M.D. but Himmler's health counsel) testified in Nuremberg that euthanasia remained on Hitler's mind as a resolution to the Jewish question in the event of war. Having proven successful, the personnel and equipment of the euthanasia program were, in 1941, moved to six extermination camps in Poland. Two of those camps had operated previously under more primitive methods.

When Stangl was transferred to the euthanasia program, his superiors advised him that mercy killings would soon be law in all of Germany and the civilized world. He, as a security specialist officer, would be responsible for law and order in the complexes prepared for this program in Germany and Austria, and would be supervised by the bureaucrats at "T4." T4 was the office building Tiergarten Strasse 4 in an exclusive neighborhood of Berlin that housed the "Desk Murderers," the planners and the administrators of the destruction program.

Adolf Eichmann, a high ranking official in the extermination program, was kidnapped by the Israelis in 1960, from his hideout in Buenos Aires, and executed following his trial in Israel.

At the trial, an Israeli captain conducted the interrogation. Captain Avner Less read from a document dated October 11, 1941: "I [Eichmann's superior at T4] request the promotion of *SS Sturmbannfuehrer* Adolf Eichmann to *Obersturmbannfuehrer,* effective November 9, 1941. I propose this promotion of Eichmann's based on his outstanding performance. As head of the Central Office for Jewish emigration, he has made an importar.t contribution to the De-Judification of the Ostmark."

Eichmann: In Vienna, and in Prague as well, I did my job with unusual zeal. I regard my work as a binding duty....

Less: Will you agree that any sane person reading this document will take it to mean only one thing, namely, that you were promoted to *Obersturmbannfuehrer* because you had distinguished yourself by sending large numbers of Jews to their death with the requisite hardness, and by stealing their money and property?

Eichmann: Today, after fifteen years, it really looks that way.

Less: Did you believe that the German nation could survive only if all the Jews in Europe were exterminated?

Eichmann:...At that time I obeyed my orders without thinking; I just did as I was told. That's where I found my -- how shall I say -- fulfillment. It made no difference what the orders were, Herr Hauptmann."*

This "De-Judification" had been announced at the January 1942 meeting at Wannsee, but was never referred to as such. Eichmann called it "emigration," *Auswanderung.* No written orders existed, but everybody involved in this giant undertaking knew its purpose, and understood his role well.

When Siegfried's father died suddenly during the winter of 1940-1941, his mother moved in with us. She and her husband had been deeply religious, and when we moved to Amsterdam I promised them that I would keep a strict Jewish household. They knew that they were always welcome at our home. As much as Siegfried's mother had been against our marriage in 1933, she now considered it an unusually good one, and often

---

* From *Eichmann Interrogated* [Transcripts from the archives of the Israeli police]

told us how wrong she had been to try to prevent it. Naturally the presence of her only grandchild made her happy, but surrounding events depressed her more and more.

In early December 1941, a friend begged me to come with her to see a fortune teller. She was afraid, upset like all of us; and although I did not then and still do not, believe in predicting fortunes, to calm her down, I did accompany her. I had no intention of availing myself of the services of this "seer," but when we entered, she asked me to follow her into the next room. Immediately after sitting down, she actually fell into a trance.

Her first words were that she was sorry, but her news for me was not happy. She saw me as a widow, which I took as a joke. In fact, I asked if I could get a divorce instead, because black was not becoming to me. Disregarding what I said, she asked if I knew a man by the name of Max, who would bring great changes into our life. I did not know such a person, so I discounted this announcement also. She ended by saying that during this week, a death would come to my family and that the police would be involved. This was too much, and I went into the waiting room where my friend was sitting. Soon she was called, and subsequently emerged with a completely different future. She said that the woman was never once in a trance and, on the contrary, asked her many questions.

I had decided not to talk about my afternoon because I knew that Siegfried would be angry with me for even having gone to listen. But my curiosity being stronger, I did ask Siegfried if he knew someone named Max. How did I know this name, he asked? It seems that this same day, a German "trustee" had entered their offices and announced that he was ordered to take charge of the entire company. His first name was Max, and his further news was that all Jewish employees were fired!

One day in early December 1941, my mother-in-law could not be aroused from her sleep. Immediately we took Doris to a neighbor's. While waiting for the doctor, we found an empty bottle of sleeping pills and a letter. She was too old, (sixty-three!) she said, to start life in a new country. The money for her visa and trip to Cuba could be better used for our move. She didn't want to cause any complications. She died without regaining consciousness and was buried on December 7, 1941, the day that destroyed all hope of leaving Europe. My mother-in-law's suicide, the inquisition by local police, and her funeral were some of the most crushing events of my life. Siegfried's mother had chosen her own death. She did not have to wait for her ride on a cattle car, to be humiliated on her way to the gas chamber, robbed of her dignity.

Meanwhile in Holland, as in all other occupied countries of Europe, the German reaction to Pearl Harbor had brought a new wave of hatred against all Jews. The first targets for deportation were the stateless Jews under 40. Early in July of 1942, we each received an order to appear at the train station in Amsterdam on July 15 at 1:30 a.m. for Resettlement to the East. We were each allowed to bring one suitcase, and had to surrender our house keys, which bewildered and frightened us.

For some time, the situation for all Jewish residents of Holland had been deteriorating. Our telephones had been removed, we could not leave our houses between 6 p.m. and 6 a.m., and the use of public transportation was forbidden. Our bicycles, radios and all valuables had to be delivered to special German agencies. Our money was deposited in a special bank, with a typical Jewish name. Additionally, every Jew six years and older had to wear the yellow star, firmly sewn to each piece of outer clothing.

These policies were carried out in the large cities of every European country under German control. The Jewish population was herded to ghettos within the capital city, or was shipped to a transit camp elsewhere in the country, to simplify the final deportation to the east, Eichmann's "Emigration." The trains, comprised mostly of freight cars, ran on a regular schedule. Auschwitz, Sobibor, or Treblinka, or for "special prisoners," Bergen-Belsen and Theresienstadt.*

To get more information on our removal to the East, we went to the Jewish Council (*Judenrat*) in Amsterdam. Every occupied town of more than 10,000 had to create such an agency, presumably to advise Jews on how to comply with

---

* *The Macmillan Atlas of the Holocaust*, (Martin Gilbert, 1982) offers more than 300 maps of the train routes used for deportation of the Jews to different labor camps, noting the points of origin and destination, and the numbers of people on each train.

the strange new regulations. In fact, it developed into a sinister agency, composed of other Jews drafted into service by the Germans to act as "advisors" to their own people. One of the tasks of the *Judenrat* was to compile a list of Jews scheduled for deportation. This list changed daily, and it was mandatory that the names be delivered a day before the scheduled departure. The Germans' main concern was with numbers, and not with the identities of the deportees.

After the war, *Judenrat* officials were widely attacked as having collaborated with the Germans. But imagine yourself in the position of those involuntary leaders. If the orders were not followed, they were executed. When they drew up the lists, could they be blamed for omitting the names of those closest to them? It became a moot point, for in the end, everyone was deported and most killed; but always, there was the hope that the war might be over any day. Fortunately, I was never required to make such devastating decisions.

At the *Judenrat*, we were told by a clerk that the Council itself knew only that we would be going to work and, (this seemed important) that if there were children they should be taken along, as we would be living together in family camps. Exchanging our skimpy information with our friends, Siegfried and I decided that we needed time to explore any possibilities for escaping this horrid expulsion. To secure an extension, we found a surgeon who was willing to remove Siegfried's perfectly healthy appendix. My visit to the local Gestapo with the doctor's certificate, insured us an extension of two weeks for convalescence.

I used those days to gather information and learned that any job connected with the Jewish Council or its agencies provided temporary exemption from deportation. Since the family was always included in the temporary exemption, I applied for work of any kind and was hired as a cook for a Jewish old people's home.

We could not visit Siegfried in the hospital because the hour walk one way was too much for four-year-old Doris. After getting him home by ambulance, a kind neighbor, a registered nurse, offered to stay with him and take care of Doris so that I could start work, preparing three meals a day for 40 people.

After two or three months of work, I arrived one morning at 7 a.m. to find the doors open and the building ransacked, the occupants gone. Particularly ominous was the fact that most of these people were confined to bed and could have been removed only on stretchers. Judging by the unbelievable disorder in every room, the place had been evacuated with frantic haste. I was completely unnerved. The assurance of the Germans and the Jewish Council as well, that deportees were being sent east for labor was obviously a lie. I rushed out of the house and ran all the way home, frightfully aware now of the inhumanity that awaited us all.

We had taken the first step in resisting the dictums of the mighty German military by defying travel orders. That realization strengthened our resolve to resist further threats. Without outside help or weapons, our only hope was to outwit the enemy.

Irene and Hans had, by this time, been removed from their home to a very small Jewish ghetto near Amsterdam, and could be reached only by ferry. We managed a visit, and found them resigned to their new surroundings, content to be settled down with some kind of a home. But a few weeks later, this entire ghetto was collected and deported.

At this time, families who had not been deported began disappearing. Not until the end of the war did we learn if they had been deported or gone into hiding. Trude, Irene's sister, and her husband Richard disappeared, along with some other good friends, possibly escaping into Switzerland. Another such family was that of Otto Frank, whose youngest daughter Anne, then 13 years old, began writing her famous diary, in Dutch, *Het Achterhuis*. I had known the Frank family remotely in Frankfurt, somewhat closer in Amsterdam and was later on the same train with Mrs. Frank and both daughters, arriving in Birkenau-Auschwitz in September, 1944.

The search for Jews became more and more intense. Every evening, from dust until midnight, we heard the tramp of hobnailed boots from the street below. Sometimes they would stop, seeming to enter houses and would, presumably, emerge with the victims for whom they searched. We were much too terrified to look out the window as the dreaded footsteps neared our house, for we were certain that it was now our turn. When they passed without entering, we never knew why, and eventually came to wish that they would enter, just to end the tension which was draining us so completely.

Juro, still living around the corner, came to visit and explain his family's plans. They had sent Vera, their daughter about Doris' age, to a place outside Amsterdam. He, Gerda, and his mother were going into hiding. Juro offered to arrange a meeting with the people who were helping them and we readily accepted.

We were introduced to Jo Vis, a tall, blond carpenter by profession, youth counselor by inclination. He and his wife Agaat had three children and with many of their friends, were members of a liberal church. They had formed a small group whose goal was to thwart the plans of the occupying forces, even at personal danger to their families and themselves. Jo suggested that we do as Juro and Gerda had done -- part with our child. Experience showed that hiding in the close confinement available was extremely difficult with a five-year-old child. Not only would our quarters be very crowded, she could never get outside the house. Gratefully we accepted their suggestions.

Jo knew of a family willing to take Doris. It would take somewhat longer to find quarters for ourselves. Naturally we were encouraged by a possible way out of our desperate situation. We could now take action to save ourselves instead of waiting hopelessly to be found. The next two nights, Jo came to transport Doris' clothing, her bed and many of her toys. Even her dollhouse was waiting for her at her new home. Three days hence, on Sunday, he would bring to us the couple with whom Doris was to live. He told us only that this was a childless couple who would be happy to have Doris live with them. We did not know their names, nor the name of the town.

Doris was an outgoing child who loved to visit neighbors, so when we told her about these new friends who had always wanted a child, she began looking forward to the train trip. Dirk and Stien arrived on Sunday, and after a short visit, the five of us walked to the nearest streetcar stop. We said good-bye as casually as possible and gave those strangers our child. This was October 22, 1942, six days before Doris' fifth birthday, the last time her father ever saw her. It would be June 29, 1945, when I saw her again.

A Jewish family named Safir were our closest neighbors. Since Doris had been a regular visitor at their house, I felt they should know that she was gone. They had three sons, the oldest in South America; the second, aged 20, had been arrested in Amsterdam in 1941 with 400 other young Jewish men, and deported to Mauthausen in Austria. There were few survivors, and he was not one of them. Their youngest, 16 years old, was with his parents. Mrs. Safir's reaction to our decision was most surprising and quite upsetting. "What kind of a mother are you, to separate yourself from your child?" She screamed in outrage.

For months those words haunted Siegfried and me. Had we really done wrong? Nobody could then know that the Safir family would perish completely, in accordance with the German plan.

A few weeks later, Jo announced that he had found a refuge in Zaandam, an industrial town, just outside Amsterdam. We would reside with a young couple who lived on the first floor of their home with their two young children. Their mother lived alone on the second floor. We would take our meals with her but sleep in the attic, and since this was all open space, we had to spend our days in the second floor living room. We brought our own beds, linens and blankets, aided again by the selfless Jo and Agaat. We left our apartment, which had meant so much to us, and all the furniture, and came by train to our destination. In removing our yellow stars, and carrying false identification, we were committing serious crimes under the law of the occupational forces.

We had no contact with Doris; Ab Reusink visited her regularly and left some money with her wonderful keepers. All the families that opened their homes to us were blue-collar workers and could hardly afford non-paying houseguests. Ab, to whom we had also given all our heirloom jewelry, sold it a piece at a time, so we could continue to contribute our share. At war's end, all that was left was a child's ring with a tiny diamond and my mother-in-law's very exquisite gold wrist watch. This watch, purchased in 1936, is still running and in my possession.

Jo visited Doris frequently, and assured us that she was

adjusting well to her new surroundings. She was to start public school the following year. Best of all, he brought us pictures, which showed her happy and content.

We continued to bring our friends in contact with Jo. Walter, who had an apparently safe job with the Jewish council, decided to accept Jo's help for Eva and their daughter Miriam. It was not too hard to place a child, but it became more and more difficult to find shelters for adults, so Jo and Agaat took Eva into their home until other arrangements could be made. We brought Jo to our good friends the Schwarzschilds, a middle-aged couple with three teenage daughters. He found places for the two younger girls and kept the eldest until a hiding place could be found. Paula, their mother, was deported to Bergen-Belsen, but the daughters are living today in Israel.

It is impossible for me to describe adequately the selfless humanitarianism of Jo and his wife Agaat. Time after time, they risked their lives, they cared. Their work continued until the spring of 1943, when they provided refuge for a young man who had served in the Spanish Loyalist Army and was on the Germans' black list. Two days later the Germans came to the house, searched the premises, and arrested all occupants, sending them to the prison in Scheveningen. The Vis' children were left with neighbors. Agaat, being pregnant, was released. Eva and the oldest Schwarzschild girl were deported to Bergen-Belsen and Jo was shipped to Dachau, from where he did return at war's end. Mother and daughter Schwarzschild met unexpectedly in the concentration camp and were included in an exchange for a group of German prisoners of war. To my knowledge this was the only exchange of Jewish concentration camp inmates. They were later transported to Israel.

If the authorities believed that the arrest and imprisonment of Jo Vis and the identification of his wife would end the work which they had so zealously carried out, they were wrong. Jo's place was immediately filled by Rinus Hille, who had long been active in the efforts to save the imperiled Jews. An educated, stimulating man, he kept us informed of the war's progress via news from the British Broadcasting Company, another serious crime. He brought us books, which helped us pass the monotonous days.

Finding our first place of refuge did not end our problem. After a few weeks in our first house, our hosts had second thoughts as to whether they should risk harboring us, and asked us to leave. We had the same experience many times in early 1943. People were, understandably, nervous and frightened, so the only solution was to find another hiding place. On one occasion, we were asked to leave the same day we moved into the quarters.

In 1985, at Eastern Kentucky University, I was asked this rather pointed question:

"Did you ever wish you were not Jewish?"

> Yes, I did. I don't have it in me to be a heroine, certainly not a dead one! I thought of this often during 1940-1944, the period when we were hunted and lived in hiding. But I *am* a Jew, and over that, I have no control. After our arrest it was unimportant: we were all Jews, with one exception. Sigrid was one of the Dutch women prisoners. There were other blonde, blue-eyed Jewish captives, so nobody became suspicious of her; but she was a Gentile, a registered nurse who had been with the Dutch troops in Spain during the 1936 civil war. After great difficulty, she arrived home following the defeat of the government troops in Spain. When Germany invaded Holland, she took up her fight against the Fascists wherever necessary. She helped to hide Jews, provided them with food coupons, books and money. While visiting one of her charges, the police came to arrest the Jewish woman and found her there also, but they could not decide if she were Jewish or not. It was clear to her that if she were recognized as an underground worker, she would be executed without trial. As a Jew, she stood a better chance, one of the rare circumstances during the war in which being Jewish was beneficial. The police let her walk in front of them and one said to the others, "Can you not see that she is Jewish? She has the

typical flat feet all Jews have." This was how Sigrid came to Auschwitz and the other places of our incarceration. When she visited me in Amsterdam after the war, she was no longer a strong looking woman. She was obviously depressed, her mental and physical strength were gone, and shortly after, she suffered a mental breakdown.

In Zaandam, we lived in the home of Piet and Gre Tjeertes, who became friends for life. The house was small, the means limited, barely adequate for Piet and Gre and their two babies. They had no spare room or extra bed, but they gave us their mattress, since our bedding was still at our first station, and we could not risk moving belongings through the streets of Zaandam. The warm-hearted Tjeertes' slept on their bedsprings while we slept outside their bedroom on the floor, sharing space with sacks of potatoes and onions. We stayed with them more than three months, embarrassed by the inconvenience we knew we were causing them. But at no time did they give any indication of discomfort. Not until the war was over did we realize they had disregarded the curfew and distributed pamphlets of the underground resistance on their bicycles at night.

But neither did they realize we were working for the same group, translating articles from Dutch into German and vice versa! Nobody in this organization knew who was participating or in what capacity and it was sometimes hard to tell if our contacts were the correct ones. We became close friends with Piet and Gre, maintaining our correspondence after the war. Piet was appointed to the Zaandam police force, from which he ultimately retired.

In the Yad-Vashem museum in Jerusalem, commemorating the Holocaust, is a memorial celebrating the compassionate acts of Gentiles during this period. Their names are inscribed on the pages of a book titled *Righteous Gentiles.* The names of Jo Vis and his wife are inscribed there, as well as those of Piet and Gre Tjeertes. Another dear friend of greatest importance to us, Rinus Hille, is also on those pages, as are the De Boers, Doris' loving parents for nearly three years.

In our next hiding place in the city of Haarlem, we found

another wonderful person, Gre Driessen, whose care for us also assured her a place at Yad-Vashem. Many trees have been planted at Yad-Vashem for the people who helped the thousands like us around the world. Unfortunately, no one knows how many Righteous Gentiles were responsible for saving the survivors. Even in countries where one expected to find no help, they were there. There are many records at Yad-Vashem about the numerous children brought up by common Polish people and returned to their families after the war. In Berlin alone, a city of rubble and bombed-out buildings the day the war ended, about 1000 Jews were alive, thanks to the Righteous Gentiles. In the village of Le Chambon, in southern France, a protestant minister saved thousands of Jews from death, involving nearly every house in town in his activities, despite the watchful eyes from Vichy. The minister, Phillip Hallie, later told the history of those years in his book *Lest Innocent Blood Be Shed*.

People in places all over Europe extended empathy and help. But unfortunately, way too few were in a position to be able to save the victims. The number of disinterested, unsympathetic, or frightened human beings was sizeable; but there was also a satisfying resistance operating against the regime, in varied forms and often under the most difficult and dangerous circumstances.

Several weeks passed before a hiding place could be found for us in the beautiful old city of Haarlem. It was a two-story bungalow, with an attic that had two finished rooms. Our hostess slept on the first floor, which housed a living room and kitchen, and she was known to all as "Mevrouwtje," Little Woman. She rented the second floor to a seamstress, Gre Driessen, and her elderly mother. The attic had two bedrooms, one for Mevrouwtje's three teenagers, and the smaller bedroom for us. Our home had a window to the street, which we were never allowed to open. Before we arrived, a small iron stove was added to our room, our only heat. We had a small closet, a dresser, a full-sized bed, three chairs, and a wash basin with running cold water. This was our home for one year. Mevrouwtje cooked all our meals, which we ate upstairs, because anybody might walk in at any time. As the war went on, it was hard for her to get meals for six people, because food became very scarce. Every day I spent some time talking with Gre. She was an ambitious seamstress, with many patrons and lots of work. She taught me some simple things, but my best efforts could never please her or her demanding clients. We are nearly the same age, and still maintain correspondence, she in Dutch, I in English. On our last visit to Europe, we visited Gre.

Siegfried spent all his waking hours writing of Germany's ultimate defeat. He saw a world changed spiritually, socially and economically by the war, which he deemed the consequence of religious and racial prejudices. He drafted a plan for economic reconstruction, a new tax structure, and a revolutionary system of public education. Rinus supplied the reference books Siegfried requested on his bi-weekly visits to deliver our food tickets. Our hostess needed these to obtain food, but since "illegals" were not entitled to food tickets, this presented a major problem. Members of the resistance groups would break into a different stamp distribution center each month and steal tickets to supply the ten thousand or more "illegals" in hiding. Had it not been for the efforts of these people, many of them with "faultless" Aryan credentials going back four generations, it is doubtful that those of us in hiding would have been able to survive.

Rinus' visits every other Saturday were the highlights of our life "underground." Not only did he bring the food tickets and books, he brought the true news about the progress of the war. It was a major crime to be caught listening to the BBC; the media in all occupied countries and Germany were strictly censored, so we were eager to get the correct news, although much of it was unpleasant.

It was Rinus who told us the heartbreaking story of Juro, Gerda and their family. While they were hiding in an attic in Amsterdam, little Vera was with a family in another town. They sent letters, toys, and little remembrances and discussed at length the idea of bringing her for a visit. Gerda with her Aryan appearance, they believed, could travel by train to pick up Vera. Their longing for their little girl overshadowed prudence. Gerda and Vera were arrested at a train station on their return to Amsterdam. Juro and his mother waited in their attic room for many, many hours before finding out, and the next day were arrested in their hiding place. A few days later, both were brought to the assembly point, an old theater, where Jews were shipped to the transit camp for deportation. Gerda was detained at the transit camp Westerbork, and a few days later deported to Sobibor, an extermination camp. Meanwhile, Juro was trying to be added to the next deportation group, which left regularly for Westerbork. He wanted to be with Gerda and Vera, not knowing that they had already gone.

When Juro discovered he was too late, he tried to arrange an escape. He was told that he could, indeed, be kept out of the next deportation shipment and could escape, under two conditions. He would have to arrange for outside help the moment he left the building. Further, and undoubtedly harder for him, he would have to go without his mother, because the necessary escape route would be too difficult for her. One of our friends was available to help him on the outside and he made his way through stairways, over roofs and along fire escapes, alone.

I had to leave our attic room twice. I developed tooth aches and was brought to a dentist, who was informed of my status and advised pulling the tooth. The dentist was obviously upset when the root broke and he had to cut out the pieces. He became more and more frightened, and wanted me out of his office as soon as possible. Two days later I hemorrhaged dangerously. When the dentist was called, he suggested I see a regular M.D., for the problem could not possibly be caused by the tooth and must be from another ailment. An internist who was willing to see me discovered that the dentist, in his growing fears, had not stitched the incision. This, coupled with my abnormally high blood pressure, had caused the hemorrhage. He recommended a diet of fruit and dairy products, no meats, and if he had not been so serious I truly would have laughed. He obviously understood little about our situation!

I have to confess that, unlike Siegfried, I had been an addicted smoker since 17. How self-centered I was! In the confines of our small room, I continued to smoke, never being able to open the window. With one cigarette ticket, you could purchase one package of 20 cigarettes per week. With Siegfried's coupon from his ration ticket package, I had 40 cigarettes weekly, plus butts. Out of three butts I rolled another cigarette. It must have been difficult for Siegfried to live in this stench and never complain, and my feelings of guilt remain today.

In July or early August, 1944, Rinus came on one of his bi-weekly visits to tell us what he had heard on the BBC network. He had news of extermination camps in Poland, which were different from the concentration camps in Germany, Austria and the occupied countries. We understood that there were 12,000 forced-labor and concentration camps throughout central Europe, but that Poland had six extermination camps, whose only purpose was to cleanse the world of the unwanted. They named Jews, gypsies, the Polish intelligensia, Slavs in general, Jehovah's Witnesses, homosexuals...the list seemed endless. These extermination camps were working day and night for the sole purpose of gassing prisoners and cremating their bodies. I learned later that two of the six, Treblinka and Sobibor, names unknown to us at the time, were demolished by the prisoners.

Rinus talked of Auschwitz, a name unknown to most, which housed many camps, enormous factories, and forced labor camps. There was a separate section called Birkenau, center of the most sophisticated methods for expedient destruction of human bodies. It was estimated that two million Jews had been killed here thus far. We believed all such reports, but when Rinus related that Great Britain *and* the United States had been informed of the existence of these camps, we refused to believe it. We were certain the Allies would have done something to save those people. It was unthinkable that the world would turn its head from blatant genocide.

On June 6, 1944, the best news of all arrived; the invasion by the Allies of the French Atlantic coast, D-Day. Hearing of their success, we were certain that the victorious armies would soon cross into Belgium and Holland, and we would be free.

Friday, August 25, 1944, the Allies liberated Paris. While thousands of people could then breathe easier, we could not. On this morning, four men in plain clothes came to our hiding place. They were Gestapo (secret police) officers, two Dutch and two Germans. Two of them stayed downstairs, one at the

The coveted exemption stamp issued at Amsterdam. "Owner of this identification is, until further notice, free from work conscription." Below, The Werk Kratzau pin.

Doris in 1943, during the stay wth her foster parents, Dirk and Stien DeBoer.

Receipt from the SS for removing all furniture from our home. "To present at the Bank Lippman, Rosenthal & Co. as proof that the inventory of the house, Amsterdam, Herculesstraat 3, was taken over by me," October 14, 1943. (Signed SS Captain).

Einsatzstab Reichsleiter Rosenberg
für die besetzten Gebiete
Hauptarbeitsgruppe Niederlande

Amsterdam, den 14.10.1943
Feinengracht 556
Telefon 95 745
Ma.

Der Leiter

Herrn
A.W. Rensinx,
Amsterdam
Zwanenburgwal 51-hs

Zur Vorlage bei dem Bankhaus Lippmann, Rosenthal & Co.
bestätige ich, dass von mir das Inventar des Hauses
A'dam, Herculesstraat 3-II
am 29.6.43 übernommen worden ist.

SS-Sturmbannführer

front door and one at the back, while two came upstairs to the attic. They knocked on our door and walked in brandishing identification and announcing that they were police officers with the order to arrest us. They looked through our few belongings, and suggested that we take some warm clothing because where we were going, the weather would be cold. While one of the men took Siegfried outside the room to search him, I asked the other if I could give him money or anything else to leave us alone. Siegfried and I had belts inside our clothing, where we carried larger amounts of money, from Ab's sale of our jewelry. The officer with me was obviously unhappy that he could not make a deal, apologizing that this was impossible because of the three officers with him. "You cannot trust anybody in this kind of work," he whispered. Surprisingly, his companion did not discover Siegfried's money belt.

Searching further, they found a picture of Doris that Rinus had brought not too long ago. "If this is your child, or if you have more children in hiding, we advise you to take them along," they suggested. "You will be going to live in a family camp, and while you are working, the children will be cared for." Later I learned that "head-money" was paid for every Jew, not only to those who informed, but also to guards who delivered them. Recalling similar suggestions from the Jewish Council more than two years earlier, we declined to respond to our captors. We took no clothing, since we knew where we were headed, and were already hoping for a chance to escape. Should that moment come, anything you carried was unnecessary ballast.

A student where we were lecturing at Centenary College in Louisiana in 1984 asked,

> *"If you had followed the suggestions of the officers*
> *who arrested you, to take your daughter along,*
> *would not the people who were hiding her also*
> *have been punished?*

> Very likely that would have happened. We never considered taking her from her secure place into the unknown.

On the way downstairs to the car, I kissed Gre goodbye and

pressed in her hand a pin in the shape of a coral branch. It had been a gift from my mother-in-law, given to her by her husband on their honeymoon in Florence. Mevrouwtje and the girls were not to be seen. We were brought to Gestapo headquarters in Amsterdam and interrogated separately. Our captors wanted information about the ring of people who obviously were supporting us. Neither of us answered those questions, so the threats and pressured interrogations went on until late night, but none of our friends were arrested. They themselves went into hiding for days because all too often, the pressured questioning confused and tired the victims, and they made statements incriminating others in the network.

After spending two nights in the Amsterdam city prison, Jewish men and women were separated into large groups. If they knew about the extermination camps, if the name Auschwitz meant anything to them, they did not say. No one talked about the future or speculated on the plans of the Nazis. Many women prayed quietly or talked softly with each other. I talked with an 80-year-old lady who had also been discovered in hiding. She was the widow of a very well-known Austrian politician, a Social Democrat, and one of her sons had, for the past seven years, been in Dachau, Buchenwald and Auschwitz. After I came to the United States in early 1947, I met a woman who knew this Mrs. Kautsky's son. She gave me his San Francisco address, as I wanted to tell him about my meeting with his mother. I was sure she had been killed, like all the older people that night we arrived, and that he would appreciate knowing how she was physically and mentally when I had met her. To my astonishment, the son wrote that his mother had been helped at the train ramp by somebody who knew her, that she was brought to what was called a "hospital" and cared for until she died a natural death in December, 1944. Auschwitz could bring the most unbelievable changes of situations, both good and bad! The son became an instructor of science at one of the finest universities in this country.

Every occupied country had its *Durchgangslager*, where Jews were sent after being collected. Camp Westerbork was established in October 1939, but had been officially approved for

German refugees by the Dutch government in February of that year, before the outbreak of the war. It was there that nearly a quarter of the passengers of the German liner *St. Louis* were delivered, after its fruitless voyage to Cuba. Westerbork became a police transit camp, an ominous collecting station for Auschwitz, Sobibor, etc. Jewish citizens were registered with the German police and the so-called "Jewish Emigration Department," while the occupational government continued reports that all Dutch or alien Jews would be evacuated. Rumors about the destination were everywhere; nobody knew the full truth and nobody would have believed the reality.

Westerbork filled in a short time with Jews from all over the country, from work camps and prisons. German SS officers were in charge, but the Jewish Council was responsible for order in the enormous camp. The Council arranged for food, hospital and medical care, and schools, and it also scheduled the loading of the trains, which began running every Tuesday like clock-work, with at least 1000 Jews on each. The German Jews, beginning with those who had come on the *St. Louis*, worked under SS supervision in many important departments and were responsible for far-reaching decisions. Since communication between the German Nazis and the German prisoners was easier for the people in charge, more and more obligations were added to the German Jews burdens. Feelings of national hostility broke out, despite the fact that all the prisoners were Jewish! Open hostilities were common, even though the enemy was the one who stood to gain from the fighting.

By July 15, 1942, the official deportations had started, and more were scheduled for every night that week. We were supposed to have been on that first deportation, but had gone underground after contact with the resistance group. As the days passed, more and more people seemed to follow our example, and did not show up. Once the deportations began, there was no more ambiguity about the train rides. The Germans raided homes and farms for Jews every night, filling the trains with those or other Westerbork inmates to keep the machinery going.

At Kodiak College in Alaska in 1984, a student asked,

"How can you say that nothing was done, regarding the exterminations which started in 1941? We invaded, didn't we?"

Yes, the invasion of central Europe did happen, but in June of 1944. The gassings and executions were then still in full swing; and the war was not over for most of us until April or May, 1945.

It is estimated that about 140,000 Jews lived in Holland when the Germans invaded the country. Of those, approximately 20,000 went into hiding, half of whom were captured and deported. When frightened Jews came to the Jewish Council for advice on going underground, the staff was ordered to say that since not everybody could hide, nobody must. In mixed marriages, the Jewish partner was ordered to work, some were evacuated and others not. The German law was vague on this point, and local authorities made most decisions.

From my own experience, as well as from reading and listening to reports of other women in the camp, I am convinced that the Jewish Councils were compelled to supervise the extinction of their own people. They rationalized by saying it helped keep their people from having to have so much direct contact with the dreaded German SS. This was one of the most satanic methods of the Nazi regime, but it also kept every member of the Jewish Council safe for the moment, by assignment of the "exemption stamp." The stamp read "Owner of this document is exempt from work mobilization until further notice."

When the trains finally stopped running, September 5, 1944, the 120,000 Jewish prisoners who had passed through Westerbork were gone. The camp was left with 300 prisoners. By war's end, it was back to 950 inmates, primarily people who had been discovered in their hiding places.

In the late evening of August 27, 1944, in the darkness of wartime blackout, a streetcar brought all of us to the train station. From there, a train took us to Westerbork, where there were thousands of Jewish prisoners, hoping to stay until the end of the war. There was a hospital, and many clean but crowded barracks. Men and women were separated, children staying with their mothers. At tables in the barracks, families could take their meals together. I saw not a single German guard or soldier, only Jewish men and women in green uniforms called "camp police." The spirit was surprisingly high and hopeful, and we met some old friends with whom we had lost touch. Two of them -- Walter (Miriam's father) and Werner Goldschmidt (husband of the oldest Schwarzschild girl) -- did not return.

In the early morning hours of September 3, our name was called over the barrack loudspeaker to report very early to the train station (I have forgotten the exact time). Some of the old friends came when they heard, and offered to bring us blankets and other items. No one realized that in the last two to three days, British radio had broadcast the pre-planned order that Holland's railroad workers should go on strike, for the allies planned an attack on the southern flank of Holland. Naturally, German intelligence knew about those preparations and radio messages, and decided its first priority was to deport thousands of Jews out of Westerbork to the East. In three days the camp was emptied, with only 300 Jews allowed to remain. Who decided which ones would be allowed to stay, and who would go to the various camps in this short time?

We were in the first train, which left on September 3. The train of completely empty cattle cars seemed unbelievably long. Soon, every car was jammed with young children, babies, old men and women, and obviously sick people, all that could fit. There was no seating and no room to sit on the floor; we had to stand, body against body. The luggage took up some badly needed room, because everybody but us had some belongings with him. Since there was no air and there were no openings in the doors, it was dark and uncomfortable. Only a small bucket was available for toilet purposes and it quickly became impossible to find a few inches room to squeeze to this bucket. Restless people called out for the guards, but no one ever answered. On the way into the train everybody had gotten some bread, and after this was eaten, the calls for water began, again without success.

It is hard to describe the situation, but much harder to have lived through it and adjusted to the growing stench. It seemed

the train stopped many times. On three occasions, the doors
opened and a few soldiers came in, not to bring water or offer
aid, but (the first time) to collect fountain pens, the second time
watches, and the third and last time money. They told us that
Dutch money was worthless at our destination and it must be
handed over to them.

> When I talk about my experiences in our
> lectures, I mention the inhuman and brutal
> situations as briefly as possible, for I don't want
> to appeal to the emotions of my audiences. Most
> of them already know of the brutality. Although
> it is easy to evoke pity in describing personal
> experiences, logical thinking then suffers. I want
> my audiences to comprehend what I am saying,
> to understand why I am speaking at all, and
> never, ever to forget. In describing my trip and
> the reception at Auschwitz, I do get more
> explicit, because so little is known about that
> period. It was one of the most painful and
> unforgettable events of the war, and tremen-
> dously influenced the future.

Siegfried and I, still wearing our money belts, gave the
officials only what Siegfried had in his pockets. After dark, we
took out our belts and tore all our money into little pieces and
threw it on the filthy floor. How hard it was both physically and
mentally, to destroy this money, for which we had worked and
saved for years. It was Siegfried's idea, for which I am forever
grateful.

We arrived in the middle of the third night. When the doors
opened, the platform was as bright as day. Prisoners in blue-
and-white striped uniforms jumped into the car, throwing all
luggage outside to the ground. People became extremely upset
because they saw no chance to recover their belongings, but the
prisoners assured them that all would be delivered! I cannot say
how many people in our car alone died on this trip. The
confusion was indescribable. The Germans had a way of
intentionally creating confusion to upset the prisoners. Their
tactics led to beatings and shootings, and always there was
screaming. In less than a full day, we saw the truth of the

situation. No one pretended anymore.

A student once commented after our lecture,

> *"I have read that in some camps the prisoners become restless and argumentative when the train-loads of new prisoners did not arrive on schedule. Did they expect that the war was over and were they afraid of another disappointment? I cannot understand the connection."*

> The prisoners assigned to trainloads of new transports were fully aware of the schedule. The ones who lugged the newcomers' baggage to the warehouses for sorting were under the sharpest observation and control, to deter stealing of valuables, clothing and food that nearly all new arrivals carried with them. Nevertheless, many of those goods were stolen and used as bartering objects throughout the camp. Those involved in the dealings became obsessed with acquiring an additional piece of bread or soap, or whatever. This is why they so anxiously awaited new transports, knowing better than anyone what the future of those newcomers would be. I spent two months in Birkenau-Auschwitz, but not until 1978 or 1979 did I read about this phenomena in Gitta Sereny's *Into That Darkness*.

Upon arrival, I asked one of the other prisoners on the platform where we were. There was no answer, not even a look. Men and women were separated into two endless columns. There were approximately 160-175 people in each car, and from our vantage point, you could not see the beginning or end of the train. On the trip, I had talked with a woman caring for a little girl about the age of our daughter. They, too, had been arrested in hiding and were told the same story by the arresting officers that it was advisable to take children out of hiding because we would be located in family camps where they would receive care. For a very short time I had a gnawing feeling that we had made the wrong decision in leaving our child with strangers. But this soon changed.

The woman and I, with the child between us, were in a row
moving slowly toward the end of the platform. We could see a
remarkably good-looking officer in a well-tailored uniform and
highly polished boots. A woman in white, probably pretending to
be a nurse, stood next to him. By this time it was broad daylight.
The officer looked us over and asked if this were my child,
which I naturally denied. With no other word he pointed his
right thumb in the direction the woman and her child should go
and his left one for me to follow. My logical thought was that
she, with her child, was being brought to the "family camp," but
in fact, she and her child were probably dead within the hour. I
went with some other women down a path that ran into an open
siding. It could not be Auschwitz, I decided, not the extermination camp, because one could hear voices, dogs barking, and
even some distant music. I mentioned to some of my companions that here were definite signs of life, and that where
there is life there is hope. While we were waiting, a large group
of men arrived from our train, my husband with them. He and I
sat on the ground and talked for quite a long time, tense about
what was to come. The women were called into a large one-story
hall. Not expecting that we never would see each other again, we
hardly said goodbye. It was the last time I saw Siegfried. How he
died, where, and when are unknown. For Siegfried and many
millions more, few death records were found.

Once inside, everyone lined up at long tables to be registered in a book. Each of us was given a number, which was
tattooed on our left forearm, mine being A 25254. The number
was soon imprinted on one's brain too, because it was used
instead of the name, whenever one was wanted. This work was
done by young women, each wearing a different dress of a silky,
black material. Their hair was neat and attractive, and I
assumed they were civil employees of the Germans. In reality,
they were Jewish prisoners. Those same women were with us
when we entered a large circle, formed by the soldiers with their
huge guard dogs. We were ordered to strip completely, our
bodies and orifices searched for valuables by those women in
the black dresses. One of them silently pulled my wedding band
from my finger, while another tried to bargain with me to give
her my shoes. I did not yet realize that good sturdy walking

shoes were most valuable and could easily mean the difference between life or death. But instinct told me to hold on to them, because she promised too many things in return. I realized that I probably could not get another pair of shoes, if she as an old-timer needed them. A few minutes later I heard a similar conversation between Mrs. Frank (Anne Frank's mother) and another of the women. They agreed that she would get Mrs. Frank's shoes for arranging extra daily portions of soup for her and her two girls. Need I say that Mrs. Frank never saw the promised soup or any of those women again?

The Franks had been arrested in their hiding place about three weeks before we had. They were sent first to Westerbork and were transported to Auschwitz on our train. I had known the Frank family through some friends in Frankfurt, but I don't remember having met them until we all lived in Amsterdam and attended two or three of the same social gatherings.

I remember being impressed with Mr. Frank's intelligence, his dignity and charm, and the loving manner in which he talked about his younger daughter. His erect bearing reflected his youthful service as an officer in the German Army in World War I. Our first morning in Birkenau, we discovered that we had traveled together, and being in the same barrack, we had a chance to talk. Anne was then 15 years old, 16 being the division between life and the gas chamber. Anne was a precocious and gifted writer. Her book is a testimonial to hope and tolerance, despite her reporting of a life of persecution and deprivation, for she can say, "I still believe that people are really good at heart." I have accepted those words and believe in them, quoting them innumerable times.

Parents of some high school students in Greenville, Tennessee, where *Diary of a Young Girl* had been made part of the curriculum, brought suit, claiming that Anne Frank's writing was anti-Christian. The entry to which they objected was written four weeks before Anne was arrested. She was disappointed in Peter, the object of her only teen love, for claiming no religion, scoffing at Jesus Christ, and using the name of God in vain. She wished that he would discover religion, saying that people who have a religion should be glad, for not everyone had the gift of believing in heavenly things. With religion, Anne maintains, one doesn't have to be afraid of punishment after death; a religion, no matter which one, helps a person on the right path. Ironically, Anne was subjected to death at the hands of men who believed in a doctrine of supremacy that had no room for religious freedom.

In her diary, Anne describes a tenant who lived in their Amsterdam apartment named Werner Goldschmidt. We knew this young man, and had last seen him at Westerbork. On the day after the Franks left their hiding place, he became very worried that the police would come to his apartment. Neither he nor anyone else knew if the Franks had been arrested or had gone into hiding, for naturally one kept all plans secret.

Educational psychologist Bruno Bettelheim -- himself a survivor of two concentration camps -- suggests in his book *The Informed Heart*, that perhaps the Franks should have had a gun with them to kill at least one or two of the SS when they arrived, to hinder the functioning of the police state. In questioning the sensibility of the Frank family's efforts to stay together, Bettelheim concludes, "they all died anyway except Anne's father," hardly a logical or sensitive conclusion for a man of such background to establish. In a foreword he wrote for Dr. Miklos Nyiszli's book *Auschwitz: A Doctor's Eyewitness Account*, Bettelheim lashes out at the doctor's acceptance of working under the infamous Dr. Josef Mengele, although he should have known that it was impossible to refuse work if one hoped to come out alive. Suggests Bettelheim in this instance: when you knew your life would be lost anyway, protesting as a group, using explosives or weapons, would have been the ethical and honorable way to die, taking with you a few SS men. This was the solution seen by many of those who were confronted with such a decision. But for me, the hope of life, our most precious possession, would have been the deciding factor.

Upon our arrival at the camp, our heads and body hair were shaved, and we were told to leave all our clothing but shoes on the floor. Outside, we were pushed under a cold shower. Wet and cold in the fall evening air, we were each thrown a dress (but no underwear) without regard to size or fabric. None of the women menstruated until many months after the war was over, and conditions what they were, this was truly a blessing. It was a great worry to the young women who were looking forward to a normal life after the war. There were many 15- and 16-year-old girls in our group, most of them originally Moroccan, gathered from the Jewish Rothschild Orphanage in Paris, who spoke and understood only French.

After dressing, we were ready to walk in somewhat orderly rows of five to a barrack. We still had not been allowed to go to a latrine, have a drop of water, or talk about food. The barracks were former horse stables, no windows, just a small gate in the front and rear walls. The bunk shelves were built for six persons, three on top of each other, but on this night we had to share beds with ten. The barracks were without toilet facilities or water. Pressed like sardines into the small shelves, we all slept, completely exhausted. My dream that night stayed with me forever. I dreamt that I had returned home to Amsterdam, where all my friends were gathered to greet me and wanted to hear about the time that I had been away. As I began to tell about the hurried deportation, the train ride, our reception on the platform and in the large hall, the stealing of our clothes, my wedding band and so on, my listeners declared with one voice that I must have lost my mind, for stories like this were impossible to believe. I got very upset in my dream because nobody would accept my story.

Many years later, I read *Night* in which Elie Wiesel tells the story of Moche the Beadle, poor and awkward, the handyman at a Hasidic synagogue. The war was on and all foreign Jews were being expelled from Sighet, Wiesel's hometown. They were crammed into cattle trains by the Hungarian police, everyone crying. Several months passed and life seemed to return to normal when one day Moche the Beadle appeared. He told of being transported somewhere in Poland, where all the Jews were made to undress completely and dig very large graves. When they were finished, the Germans shot them so that they fell into the ready grave. Moche the Beadle was shot in the leg and pretended to be dead, waiting until night to crawl over the bodies of his fellow victims and steal away. It took him weeks to reach home again. When he did, he went from house to house telling his story, but everyone agreed: the poor fellow had gone mad. Nothing like this could have happened. Wiesel said he asked the man, whom he dearly loved, "Why are you so anxious that people should believe what you say?"

"I wanted to come back to Sighet to tell you my story, so that you can prepare while there is still time," he responded. My dream that first night was strangely similiar to Moche's tale, told much later by Wiesel.

The night was not over when the lights came on and voices ordered us to get up. The first day at Auschwitz-Birkenau had begun, just as every subsequent day would begin -- with roll call. We did not have to wash, dress or undress, but we had to run outside. Everything was always begun in a hurry, only to stand outside in rows of five, for six hours or more. Breakfast was a hot, black liquid, carried in a barrel by four women, who supported it with four wooden sticks. Needless to say, we had no eating utensils. We were counted by a Polish-Jewish woman, dressed in black satin, who was the KAPO in our barrack, an acronym for "camp police." Roll call was held every morning and evening, and I cannot remember a single time that the actual count of prisoners matched the official number of women supposed to be present. We were held while an SS soldier came to check the figures. Some of the missing were usually found dead in one of the bunks, while others were too sick to get up. They were carried out, as were those who had died, and put on the ground to be counted. When there were too many present, all the numbers were called to see who did *not* belong in this barrack. Every barrack had about 1,000 women, and there were many streets in camp with one barrack next to the other. The women must have had reason to leave their original places, but since we all looked the same in a macabre way except for our numbers, I wondered why they would move. With us newcomers who had no work assignment yet, there was enough time for all this senseless bureaucracy.

This first day in Auschwitz opened my eyes, but at the same time made the sky come crushing down. I started to walk around, hoping to meet some of my old friends who had disappeared two years earlier. On my investigation, I discovered the latrine, which could be used by 64 people at the same time, and was often the social meeting place. I also found a barrack with iron washtubs, each of them on high metal legs. No German guards were in evidence, and there was no grass, trees, only thousands and thousands of women surrounded by high barbed wire fences, with wooden watchtowers.

Suddenly I encountered a single man, obviously a prisoner, but clean and well-dressed, with high leather boots and a black triangle on the upper left arm of his jacket. Later I learned that this sign indicated he was a criminal prisoner. I approached him and asked if he could tell me the name of this place. He told me that, and much, much more. He informed me in broken German (the only language in which we could communicate) that we were in Birkenau, one of the 40 camps at Auschwitz. He said it was the extermination camp, and pointed to a comparatively small building in the distance, close to a huge chimney, which was constantly smoking. This, he said, was the gas chamber, where many people, mostly Jews, were gassed 24 hours a day. The chimney was part of the equipment for cremation of the bodies. He answered my rather unintelligent question, 'How do we ever get away from all this?' quite literally: "There is NO way out for any of us but through the chimney. We call this our journey to heaven." This was too much for me to comprehend the first day.

Since we were never allowed inside the barrack during the day, we sat on the ground, waiting for something to eat and talking to each other. The sun was shining; a beautiful day in fall. I was talking with a group of women from Holland, which was all that we knew about each other, sharing what we had learned during our endless hours of waiting and wandering. No one had found a former acquaintance, friend or relative, so I concluded that there must have been some truth in the man's story. I did not, at this moment, share my experience with the others. Someone had heard that the "selection" officer on the train ramp was Dr. Josef Mengele, well-known for his medical experiments as well as his "selections" in Auschwitz. Most of us in camp knew nothing of what was going on around us or in Camp B II in Birkenau. There were constant rumors, but at this point we tried very hard to maintain our optimism. Physically we were still in pretty good shape, most of us having been in hiding for two to four years. The war's end seemed imminent,

and soon, we thought, we would be home. Still, we had little idea
what had happened to our spouses and were upset that nobody
in the whole world knew where we were or was able to
communicate with us.

The opportunity to bathe was quite limited. The "wash
barrack" had only cold water and no one had soap, a towel or a
rag. The latrine barrack, like the wash barrack, was open only at
certain hours, but we had no toilet paper and no way to establish
the time. I became friendly with the women responsible for
those two barracks, all of whom were Hungarian. Often they let
me come in when no one else was allowed. It was most
important to me to water down my body (you could not call this
washing), for it helped prove to myself that I was still the same
strong-willed individual, a personal victory. Washing was most
important, even if the water was very cold and you had to climb
in and out of long-legged wash basins, or, in winter, if you had to
rub your face with a handful of snow. My Dutch friends were
sure I was not only out of my mind, but would surely die of
pneumonia. I tried to explain to them how important these
gestures were for your own confidence. To be reduced to the
subhuman level (*Untermensch* the Germans called it), made it
easier for our captors to go on with their work of destroying
people.*

Many of the things one saw in Birkenau were absolutely
incomprehensible. After more than 40 years of reading nearly
every report and available book, I still cannot believe what I saw
one day when I wandered into a barrack on another street in
our camp. No one was there at the time, but I saw perhaps 150
or more single bunks, each one covered with a pink silky quilt.
Not trusting my eyes, deadly afraid that someone would find me
in territory where I probably had no right to be, I quickly left.
Over the years, I pondered those pink silken quilts, but not until
I finished the book *Auschwitz, True Tales from a Grotesque
Land,*** did I begin to understand. The barrack elders slept in a

* Author Gitta Sereny, *Into That Darkness*, interviewing Stangl, the former
commandant of Treblinka, asked why they allowed the Jewish prisoners to be
treated so mercilessly, knowing that they would be killed anyway. Stangl
admitted there was no pity or empathy when the victim already looked inhuman.

** Author Sara Nomberg-Przytyk had earlier informed me of the underground
world of the prisoners. Her book was first published in the U.S. in 1985.

private room inside the barrack, often with young female clerks. Besides having some privacy, they also had pink quilts and could walk through the barrack in long, elegant robes, ignoring the stares of the prisoners. Those luxuries, claims the author, included warm, sometimes elegant clothing and were possible if the "prominents" had contacts among political functionaries who could help them without jeopardizing their own positions.

The barrack elder (KAPO in our case) was always Jewish and was in some way responsible for the supervision and behavior of approximately 1000 prisoners. She had to see that all was "clean" and as quiet as possible, that nobody left the barracks during the night or entered during the day, with the exception of *barrack sperre*. She always dressed in a becoming black silken dress and her hair was allowed to grow. These elders were young and most had been in some kind of ghetto or camp since their early teens. They kept their distance and were cold, hard women. The elegantly dressed women, according to Przytyk, were usually political prisoners, German Gentile Communists, whose underground groups were powerful and always ready to help their people.

Przytyk was also well-informed about conditions in the infirmary, where many women were saved who otherwise would have been gassed. She speaks with sadness and confidence about the women who were saved by workers at the infirmary. The rules of Auschwitz dictated that no newborn be permitted to live, and that the mother must share her child's fate. After birth, the infirmary women would smother the baby, telling the mother that she had had a stillborn child, and thereby saving her life. The people in this underground net were required to follow Dr. Mengele's instructions for selections inside the infirmary or outside on the train ramp. But in their trusted positions, they were also able to save the lives of many, many others.

Przytyk also tells of Orli Reichert, a Gentile camp elder and extremely courageous woman, who had been in German concentration camps and prisons since 1935, as a member of the German anti-Fascist organization. A beautiful 18-year-old, she refused to cooperate with the Gestapo and was sent to Auschwitz in 1941. As a camp elder, she held the lives of many women prisoners in her hands. She was a true German and a

Communist at the same time. Orli saved the lives of many prisoners and also arranged for Przytyk to be saved during the selection process shortly after her arrival at Auschwitz. A mutual friend from the prison at Bialystok recognized Przytyk and found Orli willing to arrange for her to work at the infirmary, a place of relative safety. Orli lived and fought for the German cause and for her political beliefs, while at the same time maintaining a necessary relationship with the SS. But as far as I know, she did not survive. The SS doctors made daily visits to inspect the patients in the infirmary and decide whose end had come. Przytyk, a long-time employee, came to recognize the eccentricities of each doctor and considered Mengele the most troublesome. He was such a handsome person that he inspired trust, and the women confided their physical complaints, not realizing that they were signing their own death certificates.

It seemed to me best never to distinguish myself from the group, to stay invisible, and avoid the possibility of special assignments, none of which could be called good. Danger was everywhere. You could be caught in a selection, or in an emptying of the so-called hospital. I had no knowledge of what was possible, or when one might have the right connection. We never had regular work assignments, but were sent daily to the nearby forests for clean-up jobs or to the grassy parts to dig up sod to be used in front of the soldiers' housing.

We saw women hanged inside our camp, and could only guess the reason, if any. Another popular punishment to which I was often subjected, happened during roll call, when the figures of the counted group did not identify with the books. The KAPO and her assistants had everyone kneel on the gravel ground for hours, on naked knees, arms up in the air, with no change of position or latrine permission.

Shortly after our arrival, I felt quite sick and diagnosed myself as having scarlet fever, which had been prevalent at the Westerbork camp. I never went to the infirmary; I hid in the upper bunk, right under the roof, covered by my friends with straw mattresses during roll call and naturally all day, since the barrack was locked from the outside during that period. I recovered and came outside, after the red marks were no longer visible, for the Germans feared that we would bring them contagious skin diseases.

It did not take long before all of us were covered with lice. We were called the dirtiest names imaginable anyway, so that did not bother us, but the vermin were uncomfortable and quite dangerous, for this kind of louse carries spotted typhus. There were large delousing stations in one of the other Auschwitz camps, and it took a full day for the inhabitants of one barrack to go through this process. Everyone had to carry one blanket, which was also disinfected along with our vast array of clothing. The clothes went into a huge drum with some hot liquid, and we were allowed to take warm water (but no soap) in a bucket to wash ourselves. At the end, it was difficult to find at least one dress, and you had lost the items so carefully collected. A small piece of paper, some string, a rag of any kind, were very valuable for many purposes, but they were gone after each delousing. And why? One hour after arrival in the barrack, the lice were just the same.

During the two months I was in Auschwitz, I endured two more of Dr. Mengele's selections. When those selections came, always unannounced, all other barracks were closed and everyone had to stay inside. We heard a signal, but did not recognize it as the message to all barrack leaders. Even they did not know whose time had come. We were ordered to the camp street, to take off our dresses, put them over our outstretched arms and walk nude before Dr. Mengele. His movements were the same as on the station: one thumb in the direction of a separate room in the barrack, the other one into the barrack. This time, though, we knew what it meant.

Both times I was selected to live. But to see a mother and daughter separated, the mother to be killed, the daughter (sometimes 14 or 15) to live on alone, was extremely hard to endure. Many mothers in our group opened their hearts and arms to those children, to help them as far as possible.

I later learned that in early October 1944, one of the four gas chambers in Birkenau was destroyed by explosive material that women prisoners had taken from the factories where they worked, under the greatest danger. It was the exact time that I was in Birkenau, but there were so many days that we were not allowed to get out of the locked barrack, that we could not hear the explosion.

The third selection began the same, but ended quite differently. Three hundred women were counted and brought into another barrack. The fact that we had been counted, we decided, was a very good sign. Those destined for the gas chamber were never counted.

Mrs. Frank and her daughter, Anne, were among the three hundred women selected. Margot, the older sister, was in quarantine for a skin eruption and Mrs. Frank did not want to leave Auschwitz without her. That night, she and Anne hid in another barrack, and the daughters, at least, were later deported to Bergen-Belsen, where they died from typhoid and malnutrition. Some reports claim that Mrs. Frank died in Auschwitz before the deportation.

The next day, in the main camp at Auschwitz, we received some bread and were loaded on another cattle train. The doors were kept open and we could enjoy the beautiful woods in fall coloring. It was October 28, 1944, Doris' seventh birthday. I cannot describe the feeling of leaving this place, its smoking chimneys still visible. The direction was West, a good sign we determined.

Towards evening we arrived at a small town, high in some beautiful mountains. We walked through the woods along a creek toward a three-story building which was surrounded by fences and a large wooden gate. In the inside court, we were addressed by a young woman dressed in a skirt and white turtleneck sweater, who introduced herself as the commandant of this work camp. She addressed us as "girls," welcomed us to Kratzau and assured us that there were no gas installations here. She said that we did not have to be afraid of anything as long as we did our work satisfactorily. We would be working with 900 other women in the factory which would be ready for us in a few days. We were brought to the second story of this building, once an old factory which had been remodeled into one very large room on each floor. In our *clean* room were about 100 three-tier single bunks, each with a *clean* blanket and straw mattress -- seventh heaven! We had been relocated to Czechoslovakia in the Sudetenland, to a village called Kratzau.

A few weeks later we each received a blue-green heavy metal pin with the inscription WERK KRATZAU. It proved to be one of the most important parts of my "wardrobe," for it helped protect against the cold winter winds. If worn on the neck to close the top of the dress, it was impossible for the cold to reach your upper body. How I saved it through all the delousings is hard to understand, but I have it today, a visible reminder of hard times, and a preserver of hope.

Next morning at roll call in the courtyard, an SS sergeant greeted us most congenially. His hometown was Cologne and he asked if there were any women from Cologne in the group. One of our Dutch women admitted that this was also her home, and since he liked home cooking, he gave her the best job available: Head Cook. She lived with the other "prominent" prisoners, the maids of the commandant and the lower kitchen help, on the attic floor. I never saw her long enough to talk although we had known each other superficially in Amsterdam. One Sunday much later, when all of us were physically down, filthy, hungry and crawling with lice, I happened to see her leaving the camp, the gate opened for her by a guard. She was wearing a decent dress, a hat and carrying a purse on her arm. That purse overwhelmed me; I had forgotten such things existed. I was not the least interested in where she was going or why.

Suddenly I was overcome by a painful memory of the past, of what had been, and of what I wanted to keep buried. At night, I would lull myself into sleep by putting together a special meal, or by fantasizing about a guest house I would run. I would have few guests, but would serve them elaborate dinners -- after the war.

At Kratzau, we worked in a former textile factory, producing a small cylinder made out of very lightweight metal. The insides of these cylinders had to be shaved with a delicate knife on an electric bench. We never knew the purpose of those cylinders, and we truly did not care. The German foreman set the knife for the day and we knew how to turn the machine and the knife on and off. That was it. Personally I was glad to be out of the drabness of the camp, even to work a 12-hour day. I selected the night shift, from 6 p.m. to 6 a.m., because one extra Sunday portion of food was promised. Sunday afternoon was free for everyone and this was when the extra food ration was distributed. The problem was that the Auschwitz number -- A 25254 tattooed on my arm -- was not used in Kratzau. It was difficult for us to remember our new numbers, since there was no way to support your memory with any written note. For nothing in the world did I want to lose the special food ration, so I had to listen extremely carefully when the numbers were called. One Sunday I did not hear my number and was most upset. No one would have listened to any complaint, so the next time a number was called and nobody answered, I took my heart in my hands and walked up to take the food as mine.

My working day started in the afternoon, when we gathered for roll call to get our "Dinner" -- soup in which potatoes or a rutabaga had been cooked and removed, or a few cooked potatoes in their skins. Guarded by two male and two female SS soldiers, we walked about 20 minutes to the factory. The scenery was most attractive along the brook and through the forest into town. Until winter, I enjoyed this walk, despite the slow disintegration of my shoes. I often thought about returning when the war was over to enjoy the beauty of Paradise Valley in the spring or fall. I realized my dream in the fall of 1961.

> *"Do you feel guilty to have survived while most of the deported Jews did not?"*

This question was put to me after a lecture in Monroe, Louisiana, in December 1984. It took me a few minutes to overcome the shock of this basically aggressive curiosity. I had never grouped myself, the other survivors, and the victims in one category, whose only destination was to follow the German plan and disappear from life. I *did* survive and have not yet decided what made this happen. Truly, I do not know. Perhaps our chances were better because it was fall of 1944 before we fell into German hands, and hence the lowest times were comparatively short. Perhaps it was undying hope, or the will to find my child. No one could have mourned the loss of nearly all his best friends, and the

A new transport arrives at Auschwitz -- Birkenau. The gate of entry into the extermination camp is left, top of photo.

disappearance of millions of brothers and sisters
more than I did, and still do, 24 hours a day. Yet,
what basis could I or any survivor have for
feeling guilty? I can see none. It was wonderful
to return to the world I thought I knew.

Winter came to us in Paradise Valley, beautiful to see but
gruesome to experience. Our workday had not changed. The
morning bread rations gradually became smaller. Since we had
no knife, no cup or any other container, and no pockets, we had
to break the bread and eat it as soon as it was issued. Then we
went into the large room on the second floor that was now
empty. It was cold, very cold and we had to look for blankets.
Everyone tried to hide blankets for themselves, because when
the first shift returned, we were already on our way to the
factory, unable to guard our blankets against theft. Some of the
women, handy, clever, and shrewd made underwear out of their
blankets to protect themselves from the murderous cold, so
eventually we were short of blankets. Since no one ever
undressed to sleep, it took a long time to discover where the
blankets had gone.

I remember Christmas, for it was the first and only time we
had *meat* for dinner. There were also cooked potatoes and
green peas. The meat was from a freshly slaughtered horse and
tasted delicious to me. The soup, the daily "coffee", and this
meal were put into brown plastic bowls, one for everybody on
Christmas, while on other occasions one bowl had to be shared
by four women. Since we had no spoons, each person had to
take a specified number of sips, and was watched sharply by the
others. Of course we had no tables or chairs at which to eat; only
our bunks.

Winter brought more unhappiness. A large shower instal-
lation was built, and we were very much looking forward to
having water for ridding ourselves of the accumulated filth. But
with each new commandant came new ideas about how to keep
us clean. We would be taken to a camp, it was decided, where
there were saunas and delousing installations. This was a major
undertaking, for it took two full days to go by freight train.
Everyone had to go, including sick and nearly dead prisoners
from the so-called infirmary. The infirmary offered only aspirin,

dressings made out of paper, and, sometimes, warm water. It was feared that anybody staying back would reinfect us. So it was arranged that all bunks and straw mattresses would get a thorough cleaning before we returned from our journey. If only our captors had realized that the horrifying smells and vermin resulted from not having had a chance to wash ourselves since the day we arrived in Kratzau! Neither had we been able to change our dresses, which covered us every minute, day and night.

During our outing, we stayed in open freight cars, with practically no food because the facilities we used were in a prisoner-of-war camp. French prisoners, all quite young and unhappy were most helpful, but they could do no more for us than help carry water in buckets. Upon our return, we were completely exhausted. All the windows in camp had been open for two days, and everything was clean. But there were no more blankets, only straw bags as mattresses on the scrubbed bunks. All the rags we had hoarded, every piece of paper we had collected was gone. This thorough cleaning made our huge place unbelievably cold, for of course there was no heat. We used the straw as cover, but it was not too satisfactory. So a new period began -- and the lice returned, since the showers were still off limits to the prisoners. Very soon we learned the reason for this senseless cleansing procedure.

Rumors spread fast in a community like this. We heard that a single freight car containing food had been sent to camp by the International Red Cross! Even harder to believe, Sunday afternoon we were called to roll in the court and were given a handful of white sugar. Of course everyone's hands were filthy, but this was the only means of distribution, since we had no containers or paper. We greedily licked the sugar before we were even back in our bunks. Amazingly, we were also given one already-opened can of sardines for every two women, which we ate with our filthy hands as well. But this food was much too rich for us to digest, and many of the women got very sick.

The next morning nobody went to work. We were waiting in the courtyard in perfect roll call order, not knowing why, when a car arrived with four women in green uniforms, a darker green than the Germans'. They were received by the commandant and taken to inspect the prisoners. They seemed appalled by our assembly. The commandant spoke in German to the ladies, and her words will remain with me forever: "Look at those pigs, how filthy they are, and be aware of the strong stench of these Jews. We have the most beautiful new showers here, which I will show you, but nobody takes the trouble to use them." These ladies were Swiss "ambassadors" of the International Red Cross. They walked away, shaking their heads; none of them asked us a single question.

The visit of the International Red Cross ladies made me realize how little those women knew or wanted to know about us prisoners. The guards and the commandant had described us as regular criminals that the Germans had collected in their many occupied countries, and the Swiss ladies were satisfied with this explanation. They were obviously very glad to leave us after their 'do good' service.

Years later, when the International Red Cross decided to change its name to the *International Red Cross and Red Crescent Society*, I read a related article on anti-Semitism. The article maintained that as long as the Red Cross continued to deny recognition to Israel's Red Shield of David (Magen David Adam-MDA), the move was a betrayal of the organization's proclaimed neutrality and a grave defeat for the cause of humanitarianism.

A few days later some of us were called to the attic floor. The commandant had an apartment on one side; the other side was home to the cook and some other "prominents." The commandant had a shipment of shoes and some clothing for us. I still had the dress I had gotten in early September 1944 in Auschwitz; it was now January 1945. I was fortunate to find a heavier jacket, which protected me somewhat better from the cold; but the shoes were a great problem. There was not *one* complete pair of shoes. After a long search, all I could find to replace my completely worthless shoes was one brown and one black patent leather men's shoe. Still, it was better than nothing -- they *did* fit me.

This jacket had a square piece cut from the middle of the back, replaced by a piece of white material on which someone had printed my number. I surmised that this was done to produce a visible target, to prevent the prisoner from escaping. On that New Year's night, when the guards were too drunk to watch and the snow was too high to walk through, one of our Dutch women left camp. She was discovered missing the next morning at roll call. We had to stand for hours while all numbers were called until it was established who was missing. It was late afternoon when we were released, completely frozen. The guards brought her into the camp. She had felt, she told us, that she just could not live any longer under these conditions. She had been certain someone would help her, and knocked on a number of doors until one was opened. She was let in, only to have the owners call the camp and report that they had a prisoner at their house.

This woman was sent from Kratzau to the "Mothercamp," Gross-Rosen, for further disposition. Gross-Rosen was a large concentration camp with many satellite camps like Kratzau. Major decisions and orders were issued from there. I am guessing that Kratzau had not been informed by January 1945, that the Germans had not used the gas installations in Auschwitz since November 1. On that day, the first Allied soldiers stepped on German soil, and the Germans dismantled all gas chambers in Auschwitz-Birkenau. When I was on my endless journey after our release, I was sitting in the back of an American truck and saw this woman walking alone on the street. I never saw her again.

> At Whittier College in Whittier, California, early in 1984, we were invited to a luncheon by the school, prior to our evening lecture. A young female student addressed me, saying she had never been able to understand why we followed the Nazis so willingly. I asked what she would suggest we have done. "Naturally," she said, "I would have run away." When I asked where, she had to shrug her shoulders. Despite her claim that she was somewhat informed about the Holocaust, she obviously did not know too much about the manhunts or the apathy of the by- stander. I reminded her that thousands and thousands of American prisoners of war taken

by the Japanese on the Bataan march, followed their enemy into the camp, without even trying to escape. Staying alive, I offered, is preferable to ending up a dead hero.

There *were* uprisings in two extermination camps, Sobibor and Treblinka, which put those places out of use forever. In the Russian and Polish woods, Jewish, Polish and Russian partisans posed a great danger for the Germans, who referred to them as "Bandits." Their weapons came mostly from Russia. The uprising in the Warsaw Ghetto delayed the deportation or killing of the last 70,000 Jews by one month. A city free of Jews had been promised to Hitler for his birthday on April 20, 1943, but had to be presented instead on May 19. The resistance groups in the occupied zones were provided with weapons from Great Britain, the United States, and other countries, but the Jews in the Warsaw Ghetto had to fight with their own homemade explosives and grenades.

Can you resist *without* weapons? My own experience tells me 'yes.' Our mental strength, our will to resist and to live, were decidedly successful against the enemy. It saddens me that our children are growing up believing that a weapon is the solution to any problem.

Early spring of 1945 was the hardest time for all of us. So many of our women lost hope that they ever would see the end of the war. The intense cold, the shrinking food portions and the consequent weakness made them want to die. When this state of mind took over, it was no more than two days before they were dead. Stoically, unbelievably unhappy and quite aware, we, the stronger ones, buried them in a small cemetery on the other side of town. No names, no dates appear on the graves of our friends. When I visited Kratzau in 1961, some people remembered the women in Paradise Valley camp, because we walked through the town every day to the factory. They also vaguely remembered that some were buried there, but showed no interest in answering any direct questions. A letter I had written to an agency in Prague brought a promise to look into the matter, but nothing was ever done. Even I had forgotten their full names!

So many countries were represented in this group of 300 women, that we gathered with ones whose language was at least familiar. Besides the large group of 15- and 16-year-old Moroccan girls from the Paris orphanage, we had women from Crete, Rhodes, Turkey, Hungary and all the occupied countries of Central Europe. It was logical that the Dutch women would become my friends.

Since we had no "laundry" to do on our free Sunday afternoons (for we had no underwear, and no soap or water), we gathered on four bunks to talk. Gradually, fewer and fewer women participated in these gatherings. But one afternoon we started with 10-12 women and were joined by more when they heard our topic. Most of us were married and had small children in hiding. The question arose, 'When the war is over and we are free, what would be harder to endure -- if our husbands did not return or if we did not find our children?' It is hard to imagine now that such a subject ever would be discussed in a normal setting. But since our futures were troubled and vague, our answers were as honest as they could be; no one pretended to hide the truth. We bared the deepest thoughts in our minds and hearts. Of the 12 women in our group, 11 answers were alike. We agreed that while we were longing to be united with our husbands, and while our mourning would be intense if they did not return, yet if we lost our children, part of our flesh and blood would be lost forever. The woman disagreeing said that if her little boy disappeared during her absence, it would be very hard to accept, but if her husband did not return, she would surely lose her mind. Most of us lost contact after we arrived home. But I learned that Selma, who did find her little boy, retreated into mental illness when her husband did not return.

Those last few months in Kratzau were extremely intensive. I developed an infection on my left thumbnail, and the throbbing pain was indescribable. A red line on my inner arm signaled a serious infection, but medical help was unavailable. At my electric bench, the bottom of which was filled with dirty machine oil, there was a small, filthy file which I used to open the throbbing nail. Miracle of miracles, the nail loosened, the pus drained and in a very short time it healed -- no water, no antibiotics, no dressing.

About this time, a Hungarian woman was chosen as our KAPO. She was a huge, young and painfully primitive woman named Violet. The only language she spoke and understood was Hungarian. Since Hungarian has nothing in common with any language other than Finnish, communication was most difficult. She was a prisoner like the rest of us, but she took her job very seriously. She became very angry and excited when her orders were not followed, despite the language barrier, and her solution was to hit us with her enormous fists, a daily occurrence.

On one occasion, our evening meal consisted of potatoes in their skins, which we had to carry in the lower part of our dresses, for there was no other way to transport the red-hot items. We each received three or four of them, depending upon their size. Violet always supervised from the kitchen window at meal time. On one particular evening, I spread the bottom of my dress to receive my share when, for whatever reason, one or two potatoes rolled out onto the floor. When I bent down to pick them up, Violet boxed my head and face with her powerful fist. The tears in my eyes did not prevent me from gathering what was rightfully mine.

As hard as it is to admit, most of the physical abuse came from women prisoners, KAPOS or not. The male guards had their own way of punishing, which never seemed life threatening. The female guards (both groups belonged to the SS) hated this location where they had been assigned to duty for the Reich. Their quarters were far from luxurious, and this small village was a dull, Godforsaken place, especially during the harsh winter. They hated their 12-hour work shifts, accompanying us back and forth to the factory and watching us work the long hours. Few of them ever talked to us; to them we were simply criminals who had to be watched.

Germany was on its way down, but so were we. Personnel and materiel for the factory had to be cut. Food for the German citizens was short and for us it was practically non-existent. We still went to the factory, but by now we were down to one shift daily. I tried always to be in the last row, so I could listen to the conversations of the German guards. Not knowing the state of the war, we depended only on rumors. We realized that the Allies must have been successful but did not know how or where, and the waiting was very hard. By overhearing the soldiers, I learned that the Allies were already in the center of Germany, and that they (the guards) were worried about the safety of their families, because no mail was getting through. Around Christmas 1944, there had been a massive attack, called by the Allies the Battle of the Bulge. At first, the battle had seemed to go well for the Germans, but it ended in January 1945, in an important defeat. I reported this great news to my friends, but nothing changed our situation; it only became worse. We got weaker, and suffered from constant diarrhea.

One day I collapsed during roll call, but, supported by my friends, made it through to receive food rations. I found myself unable to eat, however, and divided my meager portion among them. The third floor infirmary I had never seen, but I knew women who had been there, and understood that it had practically no medications. The doctor was a Polish Jew whose specialty had been in respiratory illnesses. She seemed friendly when I entered, but I doubted that I would ever be accepted since I did not think I had a temperature, and one needed at least a 100-degree fever to stay. Still, I was hardly able to use my legs and had no energy. The doctor recognized that the whites of my eyes were yellow and diagnosed me as having contagious hepatitis. In the infirmary, you rested on the same kind of straw mattress, but could get some warm water (no soap) to wash yourself and did not have to stand in line to receive your food. I slept most of the time and I could not eat anyway, so my friends shared my portion. I was vaguely aware that a baby was born one day and that the next day, mother and child were gone. Not knowing that Auschwitz had already destroyed their own gas installations, and that the Russians had liberated the camp on January 25, 1945, I assumed that mother and child were exterminated. Fortunately, that was probably not the case. I have no idea how long I was ill, but I do remember how weak I was when I returned to my floor.

Very often when I am speaking, I feel an

impenetrable wall between the listener and me.
How can I effectively explain dreams about
hunger to people who have never gone for days
on end without food and water? How can I
describe my lingering nightmares about sleeping
for endless months on wooden boards? Those
boards, loose and about 8-10 inches wide, were
supposedly covered by straw mattresses. Originally, each person had a blanket; but one by one
our blankets disappeared, and when the time
came to sleep, we had to make do with no
covering, despite the bitter cold. One unforgettable night I was sleeping on the wooden
boards, covered by the mattress, when I was
awakened by somebody trying to pull my mattress off me. I jumped out of the bunk, took one
of the loose boards and threatened her, raising
the board over her head. She dropped the
mattress, and I stood shocked by my anger. I am
sure I would have hurt or perhaps killed her.

As long as we had sturdy shoes, we slept with
them under our mattress, no matter how muddy
or filthy they might be. Shoes left under the bed
simply disappeared. Professor Yehuda Bauer of
the Hebrew University cautions his audiences at
the annual Yad Vashem in Jerusalem not to be
taken in by literature which paints inmates as
heroes. Most people behaved poorly in the
camps. They stole bread from their fellow
inmates and reported others to the KAPO when
it was to their advantage. Life was so grim, there
was simply no room for heroics.

The rumor that all inhabitants of the camps should be killed
rather than fall in the hands of the Allies proved true. In a camp
on the Baltic Sea, as many prisoners as possible were loaded on
a nearly unusable ship, which was pushed into the Baltic. All
prisoners drowned. Mobile prisoners who were left, both there
and in all Western Russian or Polish labor and extermination
camps, were collected and brought further west. Trains became
more scarce, so thousands and thousands had to walk -- as best

they could. When they stopped, they were shot and left on the road. The captors tried to bring many to camps which were still in German hands. Those camps were overcrowded and in unspeakable condition; for 80 to 90 percent of the prisoners, the final destination was death.

The western front was much closer than the Germans expected, though, and they were running out of places to drop their prisoners. The Allied armies, especially the American troops, were marching east into the heart of Germany, spreading in many different directions. The Allied soldier was nearly ignorant of the crimes in these camps, either the extermination camps or the more than 12,000 concentration and labor camps of all sizes in Germany. The locations of these camps were unknown to all but those with a connection to them. The fact that they were scattered on many side roads or in small towns, but yet were unknown to outsiders, must be blamed on serious shortcomings of the Allied intelligence.

It seemed that fewer airplanes flew over; there were no air raid warnings anymore. Occasionally there was some kind of alarm and we were ordered from the factory into the nearby woods for protection. As illogical as this prevention was, those were very happy moments. Something *was* happening. The camp rumors became wilder and more widespread.

When the order was issued for another delousing trip, we truly believed it would be our last journey. We were to go to the same P.O.W. camp we had visited earlier, where a "medical examination" and delousing took place. The men in white uniforms (perhaps doctors), were obviously aghast to see us, all skin and bones with distended bellies, swollen all over with edemas. They spoke German, and strangely enough, like the Red Cross ladies and the guards, assumed that either we did not know German or were too far gone to understand human voices. When it was my turn to be examined, one man said to another, looking at my stomach, "She must be pregnant." My loud, clear answer in perfect German was, "This would be a medical miracle!"

We returned to camp, which had not been cleaned and still showed all the traces of our constant diarrhea, making a farce of our own cleansing. We were literally wading in excrement. Two days later, on May 9, 1945, the guards left during the night. The gates were open! The war was over!

If the Red Army had not progressed as swiftly as it did in Czechoslovakia, where the fighting went on until the last possible minute of May 9, 1945, I would not have been able to stay alive much longer. Samuel Pisar, later a principal architect of the detente policy between Russia and the U.S., makes the same statement in his book *Of Blood and Hope*. Pisar was rescued in Dachau by the U.S. Army and maintains that he would not have survived long had it not been for the rapid advance of the Russian Army. Few Holocaust survivors ever acknowledged this unforgettable debt, and it is important in view of the anti-Zionist actions of the Stalinist regimes, to keep these facts alive.

PART III:
1945 - 1947

		A.E.F. D.P. REGISTRATION RECORD			For coding purposes

(1) Registration No. ... *eules ... 1 65* ... *v.D.*

B0 0 1 79 3 5 7   Original ☑   Duplicate ☐ | A. | B. | C. | D. | E. | F. | G. | H. | I. | J. |

Wohlfarth. Katz   Herta   M. ☐ Single ☐   Married ☑   *Staten l. 'licuts.*
    F. ☑ Widowed ☐   Divorced ☐

(2) Family Name   Other Given Names   (3) Sex   (4) Marital Status   (5) Claimed Nationality

14.4.09.   Offenbach.   Jood.   (8) Number of Accompanying Family Members:

(6) Birthdate   Birthplace   Province   Country   (7) Religion (Optional)

(9) Number of Dependents: Katz Siegfried.   Nussbaum. Betty.

    (10) Full Name of Father   (11) Full Maiden Name of Mother

(12) Desired Destination   (13) Last Permanent Residence or Residence January 1, 1938.

Amsterdam   Herkulesstr 3   Lic 12.

City or Village   Province   Country   City or Village   Province   Country

               gevangene.

(14) Usual Trade, Occupation or Profession   (15) Performed in What Kind of Establishment   (16) Other Trades or Occupations

            (18) Do You Claim to be a Prisoner of War

a. Holl.   b. Deutsch.   c.

(17) Languages Spoken in Order of Fluency   Yes ☐ No ☐   (19) Amount and Kind of Currency in your Possession

(20) Signature of Registrant: ✗ Herta Wohlfarth   (21) Signature of Registrar   Date 10.6.45   Assembly Center No. N.21.

(22) Destination or Reception Center: R.V.C. Ehr.

    Name or Number   City or Village   Province   Country

(23) Code for Issue	1	2	3	4	5	6	7	8	9	10	11	12	13	14	15	16	17	18	19	20	21	22	23	24	25	26	27	28

(24) Remarks

Kratzau.
Leipzig.

DP-2
16—30781-1

Displaced person's record of registration upon return to Holland.

We were on our own, with nobody to tell us what to do! I had no initiative to do anything for the first hours, especially when I saw women running into the offices, destroying papers which could have been very important later. While they searched through the kitchen and former living quarters of the commandant, I sat on a stump, enjoying the beautiful sunshine. When I got over the first excitement, I was extremely hungry and decided to walk through the open gate. Under the first large tree I found lilies of the valley in bloom. These delicate little flowers awakened my interest in living, and I started to walk to the village. My first stop was at the butcher shop we had seen so often on our walks to the factory. Sometimes I had seen sausages hanging in this window and had dreamed of eating one. I entered the store and asked if the butcher might have something I could eat, perhaps a sausage. He denied having anything and paid no more attention to me, so on I went to the center of the village. A Russian soldier was standing on the sidewalk, a piece of dark bread in his right hand and a roasted leg of chicken in the other. Mesmerized, I walked straight up to him, pointing to my stomach and my mouth. There was no need for words. Before taking a bite, he gave me all he had. It tasted delicious, but during the night, I got very sick. This had been too much for a beginning.

The next morning, the second day of freedom, Russian soldiers set up a soup kitchen. Communication was difficult to impossible, but we had a wonderful, secure feeling. The director of the factory came to talk to us in the courtyard. He was wearing a business suit, no uniform or swastika. He thanked us for our work during our stay at Kratzau! His suggestion was, that since we came from so many different countries, we wait for the International Red Cross to arrange transportation to our respective homes. I did not believe a word this man said. He was one of the so-called German trustees, who had been put in charge of a business or industry that the Germans felt should be Aryanized. The work forces were supplied on order from Auschwitz, and they paid the SS a pittance for feeding and keeping the slave labor force. The SS in turn, overcharged for the "food and medical care." Did this man not know that while we were working our 12-hour shifts, with only one 30-minute break, the few German foremen and our guards disappeared? Never were we offered a drop of water or a crumb of food. Did he not realize that daily we went more than 13 hours without food; that it was not possible to save and carry the tiny bread ration we had received at 5 a.m. the day before? Naturally the factory workers must have hated to stand close to us to service the machines, for our bodies and clothing were filthy, smelly and covered with lice. And here was this man thanking us!

In considering the past "sacrifices" of the International Red Cross ladies, I decided they would never be of any help, and I was anxious to get going. I did not know where Kratzau was located or which way was home, but one thought pulled me: Doris. I was as impatient and independent as before, only now without logic or the ability to think clearly. Not even taking into consideration my own fragile condition, I just decided to go. I later learned that the International Red Cross did come, about three or four weeks after the end of the war, to care for the women who were still there.

On May 10, the second day of our newly acquired freedom, I had an experience which influenced my later life in an important way. The village of Kratzau in the Sudetenland had, at that time, a primarily pro-German population. When the factory shifts changed, the streets were nearly always empty, for nobody wanted to look voluntarily at hundreds of unattractive and unappetizing skeletons. What people don't actually see, cannot see them, and so does not exist, these people apparently figured. We all accepted that fact; it was just another aspect of our daily existence.

But on May 10, many of us at last reacted differently. Some of the women, overwhelmed by their freedom, streamed to-wards the village, into the middle and lower class homes, and took whatever fell into their hands. They returned to camp, loaded with "things" which could not possibly be kept or transported home, wherever home was now. One woman stood out in my memory, for she was carrying a doll carriage, for a child who was perhaps in hiding, or more likely had been killed. For the first time I encountered vengeance and senseless hate, became aware of what those emotions can do and how they destroy what is human in us.

Memories of that day have helped me find the only way to deal with my past. After I had studied, learned to understand and balance my own emotions, it became clear to me that I had a responsibility and a duty as a survivor to be a reporting witness. There are never enough survivors willing to speak out, and soon no witnesses will be alive. I knew also that the reports and explanations must be as unemotional as possible; without revenge or hate -- only facts.

Not having the patience to wait, I left the next day, May 12. The evening before, I had told our group that I would be leaving for home the next day. They could not believe that I was doing this. Nobody wanted to join me; they preferred to wait. Suddenly 16-year-old Becky, also from Amsterdam, with whom I had had little contact during our stay at Kratzau, insisted on going with me. It was not what I wanted, and I told her truthfully I had no idea how to embark on this travel adventure, since I did not even know where we were. But because I was 20 years older and spoke German, she trusted me. She was a homesick, inexperienced child who wanted to be with her mother.

The next morning, carrying a small basket between us with a few "gifts" from the group, like a flower or an onion, we started on our way. I first decided to go to the City Hall to get some kind of identification, for besides having no money, we had no papers. They provided us with a piece of paper on which they wrote our names in Czech, asking anybody to be of assistance if needed. I still have this document, which proved to be of little value after a short distance, because no one could read the language. We headed west, only to learn at the train station that no trains had run for days and no one could say when to expect a change. By this time, we would not have returned to the camp for anything, although I was quite uncomfortable at not knowing what to do. Becky, with little more than her camp experience, asked every 10-15 minutes, "Where are we going now?" We walked out of town through attractive meadows to the village of Engelsberg (Mountain of Angels). And what now, asked Becky. As if I had never done anything but guide such expeditions, I told her that we would sit on the grass in the center of town. I assumed that some women would be curious enough to ask who we were and if they could help us. Finally, I asked one woman if she could help us find some warm water to clean up, a place to sleep, and some food. The trains, I hoped, would be running the next day.

I still was not aware that all of central Europe had been involved in the fighting, that the cities and towns were mostly rubble, that there was no train travel, no electricity, and that all bridges had been destroyed. I also did not realize that the Germans had long been short of workers, and had picked up men and women on the streets in all the occupied countries to work in the slave labor camps. All those people were on the road just as we were, trying to get home. We had joined the largest population movement ever in Europe.

We were led to a home where our hostess asked us if we liked chicken. What a question! She then told us that this chicken had just died and that she would prepare it for us if we wanted. It was a great treat, and we did not get sick! Neither our hostess nor another female guest joined our meal, but the other young woman started to talk. She had been an SS guard at a women's camp close to Kratzau, I believe Trautenau. She wanted us to help her by telling the Russians that she had not been a guard at that camp. What naivete! Because the Russians had liberated us, were they assumed to be our friends? That we could not speak a word of Russian apparently never entered her mind. Because everybody feared the Russian occupation, we were suddenly thought to be powerful enough to protect those Germans.

My relationship with Becky developed as mother-daughter. I had to make decisions for two in unknown situations, when I was hardly able to decide anything for myself. But I felt responsible for this child. The next day we went again to the local train station and were told that perhaps the following day we could board a train in the next village. No one knew where the train was bound and I did not care, as long as we went west.

We spent the day walking leisurely to the village, the name of which I have forgotten, and on the way we begged for bread and water. We were very satisfied with this food; simply to feel no hunger or thirst was a most welcome experience. We spent the night under a table in the small waiting room at the train station, sleeping peacefully. That afternoon a train arrived, stopped shortly and we jumped on, found an upholstered seat and settled down for another night. In the middle of the night the train stopped; it was pitch dark and we heard men speaking an unknown language. Russian soldiers entered with flash lights in their hands, feeling our wrists and searching our faces. They pushed aside our Czech identification and seemed to be finished with their visit. I was reminded of Day #1 when I encountered the Russian soldier and pointed at my stomach and my mouth. One soldier searched in his knapsack and found a can of fish, which he offered to us with a bright smile. Without an opener it was worthless to us, but we were grateful nevertheless. Then I saw something unusual: his arms were covered with wrist watches. Later, when I heard more about these train inspections, I understood, but at the time it was most confusing. The Russians were looking for German men, to collect them for their labor camps. They took their watches, just like the Germans had taken ours. By feeling our wrist bones they established that we were women.

On May 15, we arrived in Ceska Lipa, walked around the town and collected some bread, because there was another train expected the next day. That night we slept on a table in the station waiting room, and the following day a train did come that took us to Decin, today the border town between Czechoslovakia and East Germany. We walked across the River Elbe to Boletice, to another train station. While approaching this building we saw what appeared to be a *Fata Morgana*, a mirage. Eleven men were dressed in the uniform of the Dutch mailman, complete with cape. We ran up to them, overwhelming them with questions. Getting answers in Dutch was a pure surprise and joy. They had also been arrested in Holland by the Germans and sent to a labor camp without being able to inform their families. But very soon the men lost all interest in us, refused to

give us any advice, and showed clearly that they did not want to
bother with us. What a strange disappointment! Was it because
we looked so skinny and unattractive? We found out the truth a
few days later.

The next train took us to Teplice, where we could not even
get a slice of bread, and for the first time since our liberation,
we had to go to sleep hungry again, which was very depressing.
Becky and I shared all, the highs and the lows, the corners for
sleeping and every bit of food, not to mention the ever present
lice. The following day, a freight train took us to Duchkov. At
the municipal office we asked for food of any kind, but the
attendants were not able or willing to give it to us. Looking
around, they found an umbrella which they offered us. It was a
clear day, no rain, so after politely thanking them, we left the
umbrella outside on the steps. We should have kept the
umbrella. It could have been valuable to exchange for food. But
bargaining or negotiating was never my strength, so it never
occurred to me. That evening, a clerk in a small grocery store
gave us three coupons for bread, each for six pounds. Even with
the coupons, we had to visit more small stores to get the bread,
for we had no money.

Very often I am asked,

> *"How could you board a train without any
> money?"*
>
> It is hard to explain what confused and
> difficult times these were. I felt it was my right to
> get or steal what was necessary to survive. Right
> or not, I made everybody responsible for helping
> me out of my situation, and I did not hesitate to
> make my needs known. If one wants to live, I
> discovered, this way is the only way.

The next morning we were, as always, at the railway station,
when a completely empty Red Cross train stopped. Without
invitation we boarded, and saw car after car of ready-made
beds. This was too good to be true; we slept for two nights,
enjoying this luxury. When the train stopped we had reached
Plzen (formerly Pilsen), a city on the border between Czechoslovakia and Germany. It was May 20, and we were still headed

in the right direction.

At the station, we were informed that the Americans were establishing the first Displaced Person (D.P.) camp just outside Pilsen, in one section of a mental institution called Wiesengrund. This was the easternmost point of American occupation, but the Americans did not stay long. We made our way to this camp where about 400 people already were occupying the gymnasium. There were no beds, but clean blankets were distributed. Order was, at last, returning to our lives.

We had to register our names, addresses and destinations, and then came a medical examination. The doctors decided that we were suffering from malnutrition and other consequences of life during the last nine months, so we were allowed to have double portions of food at every meal. The people who shared this hall with us were primarily former slave workers, not too well nourished either, but not as emaciated as we were. I weighed 70 pounds, Becky not even 60. We were the only Jews in this group, and we could not believe it. Where were all the others?

At Meridian College in Mississippi in 1983, I was asked:

> *"Studies by the C.F.R. Trilateral Commission, and the Illuminati indicate that the number of Jews killed during the war was inflated from the more realistic figure of 600,000 to six million in order to promote ethnic racism. Would you care to comment on this and the Rothschilds' relationship to Hitler?"*

The figure of six million was first mentioned after research was underway for the Nuremberg Trials in 1946. I doubt very much that the Allies' judges were, at this point, interested in inflating numbers to promote "ethnic racism." To confirm the plausibility of this figure, one has only to read the autobiography of Rudolf Hoess, commander of the Auschwitz extermination camp, wherein he praised himself on fulfilling the expected daily quota: 24,000 people gassed in 24 hours, for months on end...and this was just one of six extermination camps built by the Germans in Poland.

As to how the Rothschilds were used by
Hitler, no one can say how much of their wealth
changed hands so that they and their families
could live. I know only that their impressive
mines in Czechoslovakia and Austria were ultimately renamed "Hermann Goering Werke."
Most of the prominent German industrialists
were used by Hitler, or, more often, offered their
services but never had to fear for their lives.

The fact that we were given larger amounts of food nearly
caused a revolution, and anti-Semitic remarks abounded, led by
the aforementioned mailmen from Holland. We had just
escaped death, and others had been saved from slavery, yet here
we were starting all over. The victims were the same; only the
attackers were different. This experience made me painfully
sad. Had all the fighting for peace, for human rights and respect
been forgotten already? Thankfully on Sunday, there was an
ecumenical service in the court garden, a thanks for life and
promise of peace!

Our registrations were forwarded to all Jewish communities,
making it possible for my friends and relatives to know that I
was at least alive, long before I came home. Becky accompanied
me one day to the city of Pilsen, looking for the American MP. I
thought perhaps they could send a telegram to my parents in the
United States, but communication was impossible; they spoke
only English and did not understand German or Dutch. Help
came from a young Jewish soldier from New York, who could
converse with Becky in Yiddish. He told us that it would be
nearly impossible to get a connection with America. Suddenly I
realized that I had forgotten my parents' address in Chicago
anyhow! Meanwhile this young man and Becky had a long
conversation, and she asked me if it would be all right to go out
this evening with the young soldier. I felt happy for her, that she
would have such a pleasant chance, after all her tragic experiences. She had no clothes to change into, but did have a chance
to shower and wash her hair. By this time Becky's dark curls
were coming back and she looked quite attractive. In contrast,
my hair, which had always been straight, could now be com-

pared with a hedgehog's. The young man came in a jeep and off
they went. Not more than 15 minutes later, Becky was back,
walking and crying pitifully. The soldier had driven her to some
kind of basement, where he lured her with some chocolate and
tried to rape her. She was disappointed and deeply unhappy.

It was during this time that I began to realize how little the
American soldiers, particularly the younger ones, knew about
the activities of the Hitler regime. Communication was bad; the
soldiers did not understand German and I did not remember
one word of English. They treated us like the tramps we
appeared, though they should have known that girls who look
like skeletons with shaved heads and filthy clothes are not
necessarily tramps, especially after having just lived through a
war. The young man who wanted to take out Becky would hardly
have expected a sexual adventure had he known what the
numbers on our arms meant. The liberators could never stay
long enough to organize the badly needed help for the prisoners,
so they left that part to the Germans living in the surrounding
area and went on to liberate other camps. Under this system,
many sick and starving former prisoners were immediately on
their own again, the moment the Allies marched on.

Buchenwald, a camp close to Weimar, today in East
Germany, liberated itself. German guards fled after the prisoners began their very well planned uprising. It was the
prisoners who kept order until the Americans came. I learned
the history of Buchenwald's liberation when I visited the camp
in 1975 and 1977. Masses of prisoners had arrived daily,
evacuated from camps in the east. Thousands more were being
marched to other camps in southern Germany. The general
situation was very bad, with little food or medical care.

About three months before the end of the war, a transport of
400 boys under age 14 arrived from an unknown location. The
Germans decided to execute them, for there never had been any
children in Buchenwald. But there were no gas chambers to
simplify the killing business. The prisoners at Buchenwald
(mostly non-Jewish former German Communists and Social
Democrats) were politically well organized. Many of them had
been here since the early or middle 30's. Those prisoners had

known the SS for a long time, and their leaders suggested that instead of killing the boys, they train them to be of good use to Germany later. The prisoners promised to take full responsibility, for the boys' food and clothing, and for the training that the Germans would allow. The 400 strongest men each took complete care of one boy. When in April 1945, the Americans arrived, they were astounded to find among the devastated prisoners, 400 children, each lined up with his protector.

> "I had no knowledge, at the young age of 18, that anything as horrible as I had finally discovered was taking place in Europe. I don't know why, but it just seemed that the media and the government did not care to share that kind of information even during our infantry training in the army.... I believe if we had known more about what was going on, as it pertained to the Jewish question in Europe at that time, more of us would have been more receptive. But we were not taught or informed about the atrocities taking place in the concentration camps. We saw the whole works.... And it boggles the mind when you think that it had gone on for almost 10 years before we got into the war. Why wasn't it dealt with? Why did nobody scream and shout, "Stop!" I often wonder what I would have done if, in 1939, my family and I had been caught up in this, and for all those years nobody, nobody raised a voice to help us. I would have been a bitter man.... Now people are saying, "Oh, we're tired of hearing about the Holocaust, we're tired." If they are tired of *hearing* about it, can you imagine what it must have been like for the six million -- or the twelve million, when you count everybody -- to have *lived* under it? Why are those events hardly ever mentioned? Why don't we read and talk about the warm human stories, that can support our hopes and are able to heal our hearts?*

* From *Liberation Day: Oral History Testimonies of American Liberators,* by Sgt. Leon Bass.

On June 1, a truck convoy was assembled, and anybody who wanted to continue west had his chance. It took nearly two days, and *en route* we stopped at another D.P. camp at Leipzig, now in East Germany. This camp consisted of hundreds of tents and many large brick buildings, said to house 2,500 or more displaced persons. But -- and this fact became more and more upsetting -- there were not more than 30 Jews. Again there was registration and allowance for more food.

When we were comparatively well settled, I began thinking about what I had seen, traveling through Germany in the open trucks. Towns and cities had been destroyed, leaving just a few buildings partly standing. All along the way, columns of German prisoners stood, defeated and filthy. I reacted at first with a feeling of pain; not pity, but a pain that embraced all of us. Strangely enough I did not feel any satisfaction, that this was the fitting punishment for all the Germans' ghastly crimes and for the killings, the extent of which no one yet knew.

In camp I met a man who had been in our transport to Auschwitz. I remembered him from earlier years in Amsterdam, and my first question was if he knew anything about my husband. He did not at first, and then he said he thought perhaps he had left Auschwitz with a group bound for Stutthof in Lithuania. Later I determined this could not have been the case. It was never announced in advance where a shipment of prisoners would be going. If he had been sent to Stutthof, his chances would not have been good, for this was a very bad camp in many, many ways. This man knew nothing, but wanted to give me hope.

We still were very much bothered by our lice, and went to the medical tent for advice. Eradicating the lice, we were told, was absolutely no problem, but since we had had so many bad experiences with delousing, we did not believe one word. A large spray machine was used to discharge white powder under our dresses and arms. The process took less than two minutes. Ten minutes later, all the lice were dead; we could not believe it, but it was true. Our admiration for American knowledge and efficiency was guaranteed. Only later did I learn that the powder was DDT, which kills more than just vermin.

Feeling really clean at last, my next concern was with my fragile health and the long pause of menstruation. I inquired for a gynecologist and I was given a name and address in Leipzig. This doctor seemed surprised to see me at his waiting room, head shaved; clean but ragged clothing; edemas in the face, legs and lower stomach; and otherwise looking like a walking skeleton. His first question was where in heaven's name had I been, and he was quite astonished to hear my answer in perfect German. It was still only a short time since the war had ended, and the name Auschwitz meant nothing to him.

I started to give a quick report when, to my surprise, he called his nurse to listen to what I was telling. Both their reactions seemed honest: they were shocked, and if they had not seen with their own eyes what I looked like, they probably would have said this could not be possible. He could not help me, for he did not know the reasons and consequences of no menstruation, but he assured me that with proper care and diet, malnutrition could be overcome. Did no one ever consider the psychological shock we had undergone as being the possible cause?

Late one afternoon some men came to our tent and asked if I could come with them to help identify a woman. On the ground nearby lay a young woman, covering her face with her hands as if protecting herself. Somebody had recognized her as a guard in one of the labor camps. I had never seen this woman before; she had not been at any of the places I had been. Nobody was certain of anything, yet the group had already started to attack and hurt her, hopeful that I would join them. I suggested that we leave the decision up to the camp guards and not take the law into our own hands. Did they not remember how many times they had been punished for something they had not done? Was the lynching instinct still with us? Behavior like this, I felt, put one on a level with the Nazis.

Nevertheless, *in case* this woman were guilty, I felt an unethical desire to take from her something I had needed badly for a long time. I took her sturdy shoes from her feet and gave her my two mismatched men's shoes, the brown and black patent leather, reassuring myself that at least she would not have to go without shoes as had so many of our women. In an inexcusable way I felt guilty, but I enjoyed the shoes all the same!

There was an announcement that a train would be leaving on June 6 for the Dutch border; any Dutch citizen could go. Only Becky knew that although I had come from Holland, I was not a Dutch citizen. I had, of course, become a German citizen after my marriage, and as a German Jew, living outside Germany, lost my citizenship altogether in 1941, made stateless by the German government. Still, I was determined to go on this train. Nobody coming from Auschwitz had papers anyway, so it was quite easy to hide the truth and board the train.

Becky and I were offered a 2nd class compartment with upholstered seats, just for the two of us. Awaiting us were two good-sized packages containing cookies, candies and chocolate. American soldiers were in charge. The occupants were returning Dutch people who had been taken as slave workers or prisoners of war, some with families and small children. Again, we were the only Jews. It was most frightening.

After that wonderful package of sweets the first day, we did not get any other nourishment -- no food or liquid. When the train stopped for hours, attempting to cross rivers via pontoon bridges, I always went outside, trying to make myself understood to the American soldiers. I did see milk being distributed to the children and I knew that the soldiers themselves must have food. Becky and I began to get sick (later diagnosed as severe avitaminosis) but no begging or tears persuaded any soldier to give us food for the five days we were on the road.

The distance was not that great; under normal conditions, 10-12 hours by train. But it was late in the evening of June 10 that we arrived at Enschede on the Dutch border. Holland was, at that time, in the Canadian occupational zone, so the American train could only go to the border, not enter the country. The D.P. registration building was nearby on Dutch grounds, and we all entered. The men behind the desks were Dutch and asked questions about names, last living place, birth dates and citizenship. Most of the group had valid papers. When they came to us, I answered truthfully, that I had been a German, had had my citizenship revoked for being Jewish, and that we had lived in Amsterdam after leaving Germany in June,

1934. At this moment the unexpected happened: Becky, my child companion for more than five weeks, bent over to the interrogator and said: "*This woman is an enemy of our country; she is a* MOFF," (the most hateful word you can use to describe a German). The man looked at her and at me, obviously confused. On the back of the registration record, I still have in this man's writing: *Lived since 1934 in Holland, is* GERMAN!

What prompted this betrayal by Becky, I will never know. My assumption is that we had lived and traveled together under the worst conditions for more than six weeks, and that perhaps during that time I had treated her as an unwanted child who only burdened me with further responsibilities. Certainly the conditions precluded any concern for empathy or under-standing; our only goal was to get home. I did not see what happened to Becky, but shortly I found myself in a large prison cell with three men who could hardly believe their eyes. They were Germans (probably Nazis) on their way back to Germany and they recognized immediately where I had been. To them this situation was funny; to me it was deadly serious. If I had been deported to Germany, I could not have returned to Holland. I had no papers, and without papers you might as well be dead. Karl Capek's *The Death Ship* came to mind, the story of the sailors who had no papers and hence could never come into port. All that I wanted, was living and fighting for was to find my child, and I did not even know if she were alive.

Two nights in prison brought no changes, but suddenly on the third day the cell door opened. The rabbi of Enschede had come to secure my release. I never asked who he was or how he found me; I was too excited and overwhelmed. But I was by no means free. He brought me to the gymnasium of a school building where a group of young Dutch women was being kept for deportation to Germany because they had become pregnant by German soldiers. All I had in common with them was my distended stomach! Suddenly the danger of being returned to Germany was closer than ever. The only difference in our treatment was that I was allowed to go out during the day and spend only the nights at that school.

At the University of California at San Diego, in February 1984, I was asked,

*"After your husband did not return, what means
did you use to find out what happened to him?"*

No place had definite answers. It should not
be forgotten that there were millions and millions of lost people from each European country,
whose disappearances were never resolved. The
only correct lists, as far as the deportation of
Jews was concerned, were kept at departure
time. These lists state the place of departure, the
date, the number of the train, the destination,
and the names of the deportees. As the Jews had
to pay for their involuntary deportation, this was
a matter of bookkeeping. When the war became
less organized, the listings gradually became
incorrect. Since the Germans did not house any
Russian prisoners of war, and executing them
became too complicated, they shipped them to
the extermination camps, where they disappeared like all the other 'subhumans.'

I had been told that there were daily lists of new returnees at
the Jewish Community Center, and each day I searched for my
husband's name. The second day I met an old friend from
Frankfurt and Amsterdam, Jim Ratzker. I called him by name,
but he did not recognize me until I told him my name. This
meeting was my first encounter with the old times. He took me
home to his wife, Paula, an old school friend whose son was the
same age as Doris. They told their story of how they had been
hiding at a farm, his wife as the cook and he as a field worker.
They were orthodox Jews who had never eaten the food she
prepared for the crew, but had given to their son what they
considered necessary for his growth.

Jim and Paula told me of a truck that left every morning
before seven for Amsterdam. Since trains were still not running,
this was the only transportation possibility, but a permit was
needed. It was impossible for me to get any help at any agency,
for there was no way to confirm that I actually had been living in
Amsterdam since 1934. It was already June 26; I was in Holland,
but not a step further. I decided to take fate into my own hands
and the next morning when I saw the truck arriving, I was the

first one to climb aboard. When I was asked for the permit and answered that I had none, I was ordered down from the truck. I did not budge. More male help was called in to remove me by force, and I chose that moment to proclaim loudly and understandably that I was not spared in Auschwitz to fight for my human rights in vain. In a loud voice, I continued that I planned to find my child, and that if they attempted to use force, my screams would make a lot of people ashamed for their entire lives. That must have done it; the bus started on its way.

Very early the next morning the truck stopped in front of the train station, although there were no trains or streetcars departing on their runs. A reception group greeted us inside the hall and invited us to eat some very welcome Dutch split pea soup. Next came the practical problem of how to get to my friends the Reusinks' house, where Siegfried and I had arranged to meet after the war. It was impossible for me to walk this distance in my condition, even without luggage.

Soon I spotted a man on a three-wheeled cycle. He had attached a wooden box to the two front wheels, probably to earn money by transporting freight. He was standing, waiting, so I climbed into this box and asked him to bring me to Van Eeghen Laan. I had no money, I told him, but I was sure that my friends would compensate him, since they would be so glad to see me returning from the war. He hesitated a long time -- the money was very important to him -- but hearing my war adventures fascinated him and he nodded agreement. I had never envisioned how I would enter Amsterdam after the war, but the last thing in my mind was that I would return on a three-wheeled cycle in a wooden box. This was it: my entree into my beloved city, without a ticker tape parade, flags or music.

Ab and Bep Reusink lived with their three children in their own building, one of many of that style built in Holland about 25 years earlier. It was really two houses, one on top of the other. Each house had two floors, but each had also its own entrance from the street. The lower house had an "English basement" on the street level. There was a large kitchen, a small dining room and two or three bedrooms for the children. The upper floor had a formal living room, dining room, master bedroom and bath. Steps to the upper house went straight up from street level to the third floor, a roomy, airy, comfortable home. The lower level had a large kitchen in front, with a window opening on the sidewalk. Entering through the window onto part of the kitchen counter, a few steps took you down to the actual floor of the kitchen. It was not as complicated as it sounds; you easily got used to this layout. This was the window on which I knocked when I arrived. Bep opened it and yelled, "Len is home!" The whole family was sitting around the kitchen table; it was breakfast time. Everybody ran up to me, still standing on the kitchen counter, and in all the confusion I really heard only one sentence: "Dodo is fine." (We called Doris this pet name until about 12 years, when she considered herself too mature.)

In writing about my return, I now shed many tears, but at the time I felt little emotional involvement, only a deep satisfaction with my accomplishment. Bep told me that she *knew* that I would return because in all those years, she had remembered each Tuesday to light a candle for St. Anthony, the Saint for the Lost. My old friend Juro had also survived and was daily checking the lists of returning prisoners for his mother, wife and daughter when he found my name on a list of displaced persons. All of our good friends were notified and had been waiting for my return. Unfortunately, Juro's other searches were in vain.

They prepared Ab Jr.'s bedroom for me and then came the surprise. I had completely forgotten that Ab Sr. had taken our belongings from our house four years earlier and we had no idea what he had done with them. Ab took me out in the hallway, a long, small corridor, produced a cleaver-like hatchet and attacked the smooth wall to form an opening. Presently there was an avalanche of my clothes, shoes, towels, linens -- in short everything I had forgotten I owned in an earlier life. Everyone encouraged me to change my clothing, which I quickly did. The fit was by no means perfect, much too big for me now, but it was an unforgettable and somewhat eerie experience. Ab made space in the middle of the small, unused living room, and lifted first the rug and then the wooden blocks of the parquet floor very carefully. There lay hidden so many of our belongings: dishes, typewriter, all our books, silver, dozens of items.

Another family had also trusted him with a Judaica library and ceremonial silver pieces. His own life and the future of his family would have been jeopardized had this cache been found. The children were just as surprised as I, for nobody knew it was there.

Juro was the first visitor and shortly after came Rinus. Tears and laughter, pain and hope were combined in a wonderful reunion. Rinus, who was allowed to use a Canadian jeep, offered to take me the following day to see Doris. Now that I knew she was alive, I was afraid what the next day would bring. How would she accept her radically different-looking mother? I had no plan of what to do with her, or where we would stay. I was not even sure that she would want to be separated from Dirk and Stien, for they had been her parents for nearly three years. I already knew that there were no rooms or apartments available so shortly after this gruesome war. I could not accept Bep and Ab's hospitality for too long, for theirs was too large a family. And, most important, I had no money. Life had taught me to live from hour to hour, and although this was no solution, it was the best I had at that moment.

The next morning, on our way to Krommenie, then a very small town near Amsterdam on the river Zaan, Rinus explained to me that Stien was Jo Vis' sister. This entire resistance movement had come from places near the river or from Zaandam, the largest town. With the exception of our last hiding place, we had always been in this vicinity.

I had started regular resistance work early in 1943, helping to produce underground pamphlets of one to two pages. The material was up-to-date, positive news that had not been reported by the Nazis. My job was to translate this material from German to Dutch, but my memory of the content is absolutely *nihil*. We were instructed never to keep even one scrap of paper and to forget as much as possible, which we did, for in the event of our capture by the Gestapo, our knowledge could prove disastrous in exposing other members of the movement. We never knew until war's end, who had been involved in the entire operation.

Jo Vis, the first leader of this group, was already home. He

Above, 1945 in Amsterdam.
Right, with Doris, 1947.

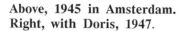

THE MILITARY DISTRICT COMMISSIONER
AT ZAANDAM

July 3rd. 1945

I declare herewith that it is known to me that Mrs. L. Wohlfarth (L. stands for the illegal name LEN, short for Helen):

first, that she was forced to live illegally (underground),

second, that she during this period was intensively occupied with important illegal work, especially for the underground press.

The undersigned is always available to give all necessary informations.

The Mayor
for him
The Secretary
M.J. Hille

Acknowledgment of illegal work (translated from the Dutch).

had been arrested in 1943 and sent to Dachau, the first of the concentration camps. Dachau had no gas chambers; for extermination, prisoners were shipped to the Hartheim Castle, whose gas chambers were left over from the time of the grand scale euthanasia killings, the "Night and Fog" program, which started in late 1939 or early 1940 and continued until the Vatican made public its disapproval in 1942. There were medical experimentations in Dachau as in Ravensbrueck, the women's camp in today's East Germany, but both on a smaller scale than in Auschwitz. Not only had Jo helped us, he had saved the lives of 40 other people. When he was arrested in November 1943, there were 18 people in his house. His home was a transit station, a last outpost for shelter. On that day he had had about 300 coupon cards, good for a month's worth of food, which the SS did not find hidden in his house. Under his care were 45 people, mostly Jewish, for whom he had found hiding places. He was incarcerated at Dachau until the end of the war, April 29, 1945, but had stayed on there for another two months until he was sure that the last sick prisoner had been removed and cared for. Today more than 80 years old, alert and active, he is secretary of the Foundation of the Dutch Dachau Committee.

In the last booklet published by the Dutch Dachau Committee, I found a recollection of an American liberator of the camp. Bill Walsh, a 1st lieutenant and commander of the 157th Infantry, was one of the first Americans to enter Dachau. He had served in southern France and in the area of Muenchen and Nuremberg, but nothing had ever shocked him as had this Dachau experience. The soldiers had been told that Dachau was a camp for interned people, and that they should get there as fast as possible so nothing would happen to those prisoners. At Dachau, a lovely, typical Bavarian small town, there was still some shooting going on. Bill gave the order to follow the railroad tracks, and when they arrived at the gate of the camp about 30 minutes later, they could see what Hitler's final solution meant. Walsh, an experienced soldier, thought he would collapse. There, trains were standing, waiting to be loaded with freight from nearby wagons. To his horror, he realized that it was bodies which filled those wagons. There were more and more freight cars and more and more dead people -- not soldiers, but men, women and children. He assumed that the SS must be responsible for this blood bath and when, a few minutes later, a young blond German officer in a smart uniform covered with decorations and medals walked up to him, his anger took over and he had the officer pushed into one of the cars, locked up with the dead.

In October 1984, at the University of Northern Arizona in Flagstaff, a student queried,

> *"I have read and heard so much about honoring soldiers -- French, British and American -- who liberated the camps after the war, bestowing honors on Gentiles who were hiding, helping or protecting Jews, or on members of the churches, but I have heard little recognition for the comparatively small group of survivors. Could I have overlooked this?"*

In the more than 40 years since the war, I have never heard of honoring the survivors. To have survived this period was only important to the person or his family, if there was any left. The one who survived returned to his hometown to witness destruction and homeless, hungry people who were also trying to find their families and reestablish a routine life. I remember former neighbors saying they were glad to see me back, but never even asking where I had been. The postwar period was difficult for everyone, even the civilians in the "victorious" countries. The only war Hitler won was against us, the Jews, and while there are many who argue this point, the near annihilation of a culture that existed for many centuries, speaks for his victory.

Logically, now, the survivors are fading from the limelight, and our children are trying to keep our flames burning. We have unintentionally left our children with many problems, so there will doubtless be no praising of our strength, our courage or our willpower, ever.

THE NETHERLANDS CUSTODIAN INSTITUTE

94 NEUHUYSKADE
THE HAGUE
TELEPHONE 7745 35-36-37-38

COPY

The Hague, November 7, 1946.

WFA' 600.

The Netherlands Custodian Institute referred to in the Enemy
Property Decree;

Seen the request of Helene Herta Wohlfarth née Katz, residing
at Amsterdam, 65 Herculesstraat, Groundfloor,

asking for the issue of a certificate as referred to in Article
34, paragraph 1, sub f, of said Decree;

Considering that the grounds on which the request is based,
justify the request;

Seen the advice of the Amsterdam Bureau of the Netherlands
Custodian Institute delivered in the matter,

Seen the relative legal instructions,

certifies that H. H. Wohlfarht-Katz, aforesaid

is no longer an enemy subject in the sense of the Enemy Property
Decree, with the condition that this decision does not guarantee
any other government measure possibly to be taken in her regard.

Thus done and resolved at The Hague, November 7, 1946.

The Board of the
NETHERLANDS CUSTODIAN INSTITUTE
(signed) Bogaardt
Mr. H. Bogaardt.

AM.
T 63251/Res/HD.

I, HENRI BOER, Sworn Translator to the District Court
of Justice at Amsterdam, hereby declare that this is a true
translation, rendered by myself, of the accompanying Copy,
in the Netherlands language; in witness whereof I hereby
set my hand and seal, this second day of the month of December,
nineteen hundred and forty-six.

Declaration of status as a non-enemy of the state, issued by the Dutch government in 1946.

Home at last, in Amsterdam, I tried to put into perspective the devastation we had witnessed these past few years, and to better understand the events of the war. Rinus explained that a blockade had hurt Zaandam and surrounding areas, and that hunger was in every house. There had been no electricity, no phone or transportation, no heat or cooking facilities since September 1944. Gradually, during the last half of 1945, these services were restored. The first actual assistance was Swedish air drops of white bread and bacon. Doris happily remembered those events for years.

Fortunately, Rinus also explained that shortly after the war's end, Dutch girls who had had relationships with Germans were collected in the center of town and their heads were shaved. So warned, I was able to understand Doris' first shock seeing me with a nearly shaven head. She did not understand what those girls had done, but all the children of the town watched and applauded the shaving process as the "bad girls'" punishment. Unfortunately nobody suspected that I might also have a shaven head, and Doris was not prepared when I appeared at the door. She had been told that I was very sick and no one knew when or if I would return. To hide her heritage, she was told that her father was in the war. When our friends learned that I was alive, they told her that I was well again and would come to her, but they did not know when. She was very happy at the De Boer's and I doubt if she ever thought of us, for this had been our wish from the beginning.

It was lunch time when we arrived, and Doris was sitting at the table, eating. She had never seen a Jeep and took a long look at this unusual vehicle, but not at me. I did not move from the doorway. For some time she acted as if I were not there, but answered Rinus' questions about school and her friends. Suddenly, she turned to me, still sitting on the chair at the table, and asked, "Are you my mother?" using the respectful Dutch form of addressing a stranger. I moved a few steps closer to her and confirmed that I was, indeed. I did not succumb to my desire to take her in my arms, for I was afraid of making any wrong moves; I was frightened that I might lose her the moment I had found her. Doris saved the situation by declaring that she had to go back to school for afternoon classes and asking if she

could be taken by Jeep to the school. She wanted everybody to
see the Jeep...not her mother. Naturally the Jeep was a big
sensation at school.

Rinus and I returned to Stien's house and, without first
discussing this with anybody, even Rinus, I asked if I could take
Doris with me the next day. I could give no explanation; I only
knew that I needed her to strengthen me. I had a strong feeling
of drowning in a world which seemingly had no place for me,
and I depended on my seven-year-old child to give me the
strength I needed to fulfill my responsibilities.

> Recently, Doris gave me a book by a French
> psychiatrist, Claudine Vegh, interviews with chil-
> dren of the Holocaust titled, *I Didn't Say Good-
> bye*. The author interviews 17 people who were
> taken by their parents to people willing to care
> for them until the end of the war. Although the
> parents' futures were in imminent danger, they
> wanted to save their children's lives. Very often
> there was hardly time to explain to the children
> what was happening or why. Many of the parents
> did not return, and often the returnees were in
> no position to take their children immediately.
> No home, no income, no family, physically and
> mentally decrepit -- most of these children felt
> abandoned by their parents, after waiting for
> years for their return. As adults, they never
> discussed their strong feelings of anger against
> their parents, even after marrying and having
> children of their own. Although this is an ex-
> tremely interesting book, it lacks an under-
> standing of the ordeal of the parents. I have not
> forgotten what this parting with our child did to
> us. But I also have not discounted what it did to
> Doris, even if it took me 20 years to realize it.
> Doris gave me this book with a note which said,
> "Thanks for giving me life twice."

The day after I visited Doris, Rinus took us back to
Amsterdam and the Reusinks. We left her clothes and toys, not
knowing what the next step would be. The whole Reusink family

made us welcome. Doris had seen Ab many times during her years at Krommenie, when he visited to check on her well-being and brought the De Boers some money, from selling another piece of our heirloom jewelry. Doris liked the Reusink children, especially the two little girls who were close to her age. Doris and I slept in Ab Jr.'s bed. Since food was a great problem for everybody, I was advised to register with an agency which furnished American food supplies, especially for former political prisoners and children who suffered from malnutrition. At least we could contribute in some way to the household! Meanwhile, the Reusinks tried very hard to find a small place for us to live, and were fortunate to locate an attic, two or three houses from them, which was not in use. There was, of course, no furniture, bath or kitchen facilities, but we would have two rooms for ourselves. Ab, always the inventive genius, got us a used heating oven and put a stovepipe through the roof. I could cook on this small, round stove and use it for heat during the winter.

The next problem was beds. To our first hiding place we had brought two white metal beds, which we had had to leave behind when we fled. Rinus, by now a well-known resistance leader and a celebrated personality, was invited to join the city council in Zaandam and became head of the Board of Education. He went to the house where we had left the beds and inquired for our property. The man of the house said he could not relinquish them, since their children needed and used the beds. Rinus told me about his unsuccessful mission, but nothing about the daring plan he was to undertake. About three or four evenings later, he and some friends brought our beds and springs (no mattresses) up to our attic. What he had done was much against the law. He and his friends had marched up to the man's house, and when the front door was opened, declared in an official way that the city council of Zaandam had provided him, as a member of the council, with a warrant to return those beds to their rightful owner. They then marched into the house, found the beds, left the mattresses for hygienic reasons and carried them out to Rinus' Jeep. They also collected the necessary furniture for us -- chairs, a table, mattresses, cooking utensils -- and very shortly we again had a home.

I was asked by a young woman whose sensitivity was admirable, how long I had been in therapy until I was able to take care of Doris and fill the role of both mother *and* father. It took more than 35 years for me to realize that I had been in no position to make decisions at that particular time, but the idea of therapy never occurred to me or my friends. Perhaps therapy was not as "in" at that time, but nobody I knew would have had the money necessary for those treatments. Therapy would have been extremely difficult, for the details of what had happened to us were not yet known. I have no statistics on how many suicides there were among survivors in the years after the war, but I do know that there were way more than expected, and that the victims used different and unusual means to end their lives.

As mentioned, I would have been the last to recognize a personality change developing inside me. Undoubtedly I had changed, as the people I saw daily were no doubt aware. All I knew was that I was functioning, that I had brought Doris' and my life into a daily routine, and that very slowly I was starting to enjoy living again. Without Juro, without the Reusinks or Rinus, the Tjeertes and Doris' foster mother, Stien, this would not have been possible.

Juro's daily pilgrimage to the Jewish Community Center to check the lists for new names became more and more discouraging. He lived alone and was glad when I asked him to join Doris and me at our daily "Dinner." It was good for all of us to have this time together and I could understand why it was painful for him to look at Doris. Ultimately, Juro was able to regain his factory, which afforded opportunities to exchange merchandise for food. Without any income, I resorted to visiting a former colleague of my husband's, to find out what had happened with their company. The owner was in New York and had started a new business, leaving the office in Amsterdam with two or three people. I told him that my husband had not yet returned, and that Doris and I were having a hard time getting reestablished. Mr. G., probably not forgetting what Siegfried had done for him, allowed me to receive a percentage of my husband's former salary on a monthly basis for the time being. I felt secure with this arrangement; for the moment I was not financially dependent on anybody else.

Soon, I began to worry about Doris. She was awake every night, crying, vomiting and obviously unhappy. I took her to see our former physician, Dr. Hertzberger, who had delivered her and whose experiences during the occupation were quite unusual. He had come from an orthodox family, who strongly disapproved of his marriage to a Gentile. The Germans had no definite procedures for handling mixed marriages, and it was left to local authorities to handle each case. Sometimes, the Jewish partner was deported, sometimes both, with or without children. Dr. Hertzberger was allowed to stay and treat the few remaining Jewish people in Amsterdam, but in secret, he worked with the Jews living in hiding, thus risking his own life and that of his family. However, Dr. Hertzberger had no answer for Doris' behavior. It was 20 years later when I began to realize what I had done, which had certainly contributed to this upsetting change in Doris. I now feel guilty for having removed her so suddenly from her secure home, particularly when I had so little to offer. Gradually, she began adjusting to her situation, but I remember one particularly upsetting incident when I admonished her for something she had done. She cried, "I wish you never had come back!" Both of us cried; she was eight years old. All of us who contemplate the past, wonder what would have happened had we handled the situation differently; I spent many a sleepless night in these unproductive probings. Such guilts stay with us throughout our lives.

As the years passed, Doris and I did establish a comparatively normal mother-daughter relationship, and I came to peace with my guilt about having removed her too suddenly from her secure home. I realized I had made it quite hard for her to adjust to me, and that I must have been especially difficult to live with, in comparison with Stien, who was loving, kind and well-balanced. This security rug I pulled from under Doris to bring her to this big city, with her wreck of a mother and woman, without home or money, was more than a child of seven, who also had war and hunger behind her, could easily forget. But I needed her to develop the energy necessary to create a home for us.

To realize that I always needed Doris more than she needed me took many years; but at the same time, I understood that most mothers have that same urgent need, without being aware of their true relationships with their children. We can camouflage our subconscious wishes with beautiful psychological and sentimental reasoning, but the need of a mother for the unborn child is mostly egocentric, to satisfy a selfish desire. Our need for a child changes constantly as we and the child get older. At first we are convinced that the child cannot exist without us and are hardly aware when he begins to prefer his peers and become independent. We forever need our children; our love and our concern for them are often the only reason that we can get a hold on daily life. But isn't it a blessing that we are seldom aware that their needs have turned to another direction? I think so, for the awakening to these facts is hard to accept.

I sometimes think about the attractive, young blonde who arrived with us at Auschwitz. We walked next to each other into the camp and suddenly she said, "I saw a child on your hand; what happened to her?" I told her that the child had not been mine, but the woman's next to me; that my child was in Holland in hiding. She looked at me without moving her eyes and said, "I knew before we were brought here that all the children would be killed and their mothers with them. I sent my children alone on their way to death and here I am. I knew that I could not save them."

I was stupefied, shocked, and felt so helpless, with nothing to say to this young woman. It is so easy in retrospect to say what one would have done, but only those who have stood in her shoes have the right to judge, and perhaps not even they. I don't know if she lived to the end and if so, if she was able to build a new life.

I became fairly close to a woman named Elsie, perhaps because we were nearly the same age and because our previous situations had been similiar. Elsie also had lived in Amsterdam, had two children in hiding, and had, like us, been living underground for two years with her husband. They had lived constantly in the same room, having no contact with family or friends. The only people who had come regularly were their resistance helpers. Elsie was not aware at first that the visits of one of these good friends had started to become very important to her. But suddenly one day, she told her husband that she was in love with this unmarried man, and that after they were free, she wanted to live with him and take her children. Although her marriage had always been a very good one, this new feeling must have been very strong for her to voice it to her husband. The man in question knew nothing of her feelings for him and never gave her reason to make plans for the future. Less than a week later, she and her husband were arrested and arrived together at Auschwitz. Elsie never saw her husband again. She came home, and we stayed in touch for a time. She took over her husband's business and cared for her children. After that, we lost contact, but I often wonder how she managed to live with those feelings of guilt.

In a final remembrance of the guilt this period brought to bear, I think of my school friend Leonie, whom I always admired deeply. Siegfried also liked her very much. When Hitler came to power in 1933, she and her four sisters went to France. In 1934, we went to Holland. Her letters indicated that they were having a difficult time existing, and that she was very unhappy. We had a small apartment, but roomy enough for one more person. So, without discussing this with Siegfried, I invited her to Holland to stay with us. Our income was small, but I thought we could manage one way or another, and I was lonely for a good friend. She quickly replied that she would try to get permission to enter Holland. I showed Siegfried the letter, certain that he would feel the same as I. Instead, he was angry at me for not consulting him, and told me that by no means could we take on this responsibility. I had to write Leonie, withdrawing my invitation. I have never heard from her again, but memories of my friend and my guilt will never leave me.

From our attic home, Doris and I began visiting the old neighborhood on Hercules Straat where we had lived in 1934. On the evening that we had gone into hiding, we had brought some relative strangers who were our neighbors, the letter that Siegfried's mother had written to us before she took her life. We asked them to keep it until after the war. We also gave them the pots we used for our final meal, and our down comforters. Upon our return, Doris and I called on those neighbors, but they did not seem too surprised (or too happy) to see us. They had kept the pans and the comforters for us, but they had burned the letter, for it was written in German, which they could not read, and they feared that it might be dangerous for them to have it. I was heartbroken, because Siegfried's brother in the U.S. would have known in his mother's own words why she undertook suicide. It just did not seem right for me, his sister-in-law, to explain what had brought her to this point.

We visited some other friends who, while living in hiding, had had a baby. This was a most complicated situation for the resistance movement. The baby was born at a hospital under a false name and given to someone for care. But imagine the bureaucracy when, after the war, the parents tried to have the child registered in her rightful name. It would have been akin to a ridiculous comedy, had it not been so sad and serious.

It was November, 1945, when we moved back to Hercules Straat, exactly three years after we had gone from here into hiding -- an endless three years. Germany's greatest son, philosopher, poet, playwright, scientist, and financial genius, Johann Wolfgang von Goethe, once said, "May God not give me what I am able to carry." We have so much more strength than we ever imagine, when it is necessary...if we are willing to take chances to stay alive, regardless of the consequences.

Curiously, more women lived through those years in the camps than men. Our work was no different than the men's. Clothing and living conditions were the same, and in many family camps, the women always gave part of their portions to their men and children. Punishments were nearly the same, as well. Does this substantiate the notion that women have more endurance, more stamina? Are we more resilient?

Time passed, with no sign, no message from Siegfried. Juro, too, was waiting for his loved ones. Juro was a good friend to Doris and me, and he continued to come many evenings to have dinner with us. With the new apartment we had a little garden, two small bedrooms and a living-dining room. Friends collected odds and ends of furniture for us, and we now had space for our books, which made it a real home. Our three glass door bookcases, which Siegfried had designed in 1932, had been kept at the Reusink's house with our books. These gave me the warm feeling of creating a new beginning.

Doris and I visited the Tjeertes, where Siegfried and I had lived for three months in 1943. Piet and Gre then had two babies, but by now they had six children. We also visited Stien, Doris' foster mother, who had had eye surgery during the war and sent Doris to spend those weeks with the Tjeertes. Stien had developed cancer and she died a few years after the war.

Our reunions with friends were upsetting, exciting and wonderful, all at the same time. I had told Doris about these many wonderful people, and was glad that she could meet them. We visited Gre and Mevrouwtje, who still shared the house in Haarlem where Siegfried and I had lived for more than a year. We talked separately with them, since our relationship with each was completely different. Mevrouwtje told me, without my asking, that all the belongings we had left in the house when we were arrested just one year earlier -- bedding, blankets, clothing, everything we had in our little room -- were given to her by the SS to keep. They must have been sure that where we were going, there was no return ticket. I was too surprised to follow through with my first plan, which had been to ask Mevrouwtje for bedding and blankets. I would find another source for our necessities. As I pondered this situation, I began to wonder how she could have accepted our belongings, knowing that we left with nothing? We had been on good terms, and hadn't she, in fact, been too upset to say goodbye to us when we were taken away? Still, she *had* taken us in and protected us for more than a year. And I'm sure the comparatively small amount we paid was badly needed by her, for she was raising her three daughters alone and lived very modestly.

As more became known about the way the SS and the Gestapo hunted Jews -- that people were paid for every hidden Jew brought to the attention of the agencies, and that lies about family camps were invented to get money for our children too --

my suspicion slowly grew, that Mevrouwtje understandably became afraid of the consequences of hiding two Jews and considered taking the premium for us. Had I really wanted to know if my conclusion were true, I could have found out through our friends in the former underground movement, whose connections were reliable. I felt bad that my suspicions ever came to mind, but they did. In all cases that we knew, the people who had been discovered housing illegals were severely punished, yet she had been *rewarded* with our belongings! Mevrouwtje is no longer living, and I have never mentioned to Gre or anybody else in Holland that I had become more suspicious over the years. But nobody in our circle of friends could suggest anyone else who would have had any interest or reason to commit this unmentionable crime.

I had little contact with women who had been with me in camp. It seemed that everybody in those early months wanted to put the war completely out of their minds. We were not yet ready to piece together what had happened. The daily practical responsibilities seemed to be all I could manage. I coped with the inevitable but overpowering emotional trauma by allowing nothing to probe my deeper self. I thought I was succeeding at protecting my vulnerability, when I encountered a complete stranger who recognized my unusual reactions. His impressions of me were most enlightening.

My encounters with this stranger resulted from my desire to rid myself of my financial dependence on my husband's former company. It was uncertain if I could get a working permit as an alien, but I wanted to try. Our good friend Rinus told me about a home for children whose parents were in custody on charges of collaboration with the German occupational forces. The children were being made to suffer for their parents' deeds or crimes, and nobody wanted to take care of them; this home needed a housemother. The story reminded me of our own Jewish children, who were taken from us, and, in the end, were killed. I wanted to work in this home; I felt that as important as the new apartment was, this position would have greater impact for our future. I worried that those children had experienced so much resentment and hate because their fathers had been Nazis or war criminals, that it would be little surprise if later in life they were attracted by the Neo-Nazi Movement.

Rinus arranged for an interview with the head of the administering social service agency. The supervisor told me of their difficulties in finding help to care for these children, and asked about my background. I told him briefly about my life before and during the war, and he was most interested, particularly when I told him why I wanted to be there. His answer was a deep and long lasting disappointment. He said, "Your reasoning, your background, makes you the most logical person to care for these children. But I must advise you to wait, perhaps a year or so, before you are truly ready to reenter the world. Obviously, your soul is like stone, without any emotions, and you function by logic and reason only."

A few years later I accepted his decision fully, but my belief became even stronger that a younger generation can never be made to suffer for the sins of its fathers. The horrendous crimes of the Nazis and Fascists, the persecution of one segment of the population by another must be examined and made public in detail. The courts must decide how to handle the perpetrators, but their children and grandchildren must be absolved. It had become time for me to take a stand.

In March 1982, while a guest on "Good Morning America," I was asked this unexpected question:

> *"When did you know that hate and vengeance were wrong and not the way to fight for a more peaceful and secure world?"*

I described my application to be housemother for the abandoned children of accused Nazis, an episode I had not considered since it happened. I told the story succinctly, realizing during this interview that my direction had been set in 1945, and that what was building within I would carry with me day and night. I knew that I would follow this conviction, whatever the outcome. Little did I know that my concern for the Nazi orphans would later cause some disturbing reactions from my Jewish audiences.

In early 1946, I learned that Switzerland would accept for a three-month stay, 300 children from Holland who had suffered from malnutrition during the last winter of the war, if Swiss families could be found for them. Various churches and the Jewish Community Center were very active in the preparations. Doris would be eligible, and I wished for her sake that she could go. The time of departure drew nearer, but I had not yet found a sponsor family for Doris. In truth, the organizations were not too helpful, and I had to try many places -- still without public transportation -- before I was able to make a satisfactory arrangement. I was helped by friends who had escaped into Switzerland, and were in a refugee camp at a small town in the foothills of Mont Blanc. They had befriended a family with three children who were willing to accept Doris for the three months. With all the difficulties involved in reaching the train station, we missed the special train sent from Switzerland. Doris was crying so hard that I was barely able to explain that I would try to call the next stop in Holland, and ask them to hold the train for my daughter. This was arranged, with the help of many people at the station, and when we arrived on another train at Hilversum, everybody was ready to grab the suitcases and Doris, to push her through the last door of the slowly moving train. She spent three months with this lovely family, and returned happy and healthy.

As for my own physical recovery during this period, all I seemed to need were tender, loving friends, food and rest. With these, I regained my strength. My interest in current affairs and in the many political changes then taking place, was practically nonexistent during this period. I remember little about the trials at Nuremberg or the beginning of the Cold War, and had to read about those events years later, although I had lived in Europe while they were occurring. In short, only matters pertinent to Doris' and my lives were of importance to me.

As time went on with no sign of Siegfried, my parents insisted that Doris and I come to live near them in the United States. It was early fall when I considered applying for visas for Doris and me. I assumed it would take a long time, judging from earlier experiences. I asked my parents to look for sponsors for us, since I could not imagine that financially they would be accepted as sponsors. I did not want to leave Holland; I loved the people here. I wanted to stay in Europe because I was deadly afraid of the United States and the beginning of an unknown life. It seemed that just when I was beginning to build some security, I had to make this monumental decision. I decided to leave, partly to give Doris an opportunity to gain citizenship, for I knew the consequences of being a stateless person, and it did not appear that we could become citizens of Holland. I could also understand my parents' feelings; they wanted nothing more than to have us share the possibilities in their new country. When I considered that unless we moved, Doris would have to grow up without relatives, my decision was made.

The necessary papers and the visa came so quickly that there was no ship passage available, not to mention the money needed for the tickets. Friend Rinus arranged space on the *Westerdam*, a large passenger ship which had been sunk by the Dutch themselves during the German invasion, to close off the harbor. It had been retrieved from the ocean bottom and completely restored, the first passenger ship to sail from Holland to the United States after the war. I would be able to get two tickets *if* I could pay for them. I had never asked for help from any organization after the war, so I thought I was justified in approaching a Jewish agency for the first time. It was also my last time!

After filling out the necessary forms, I was told that there was only one small formality. They would need my father's signature as the responsible party for his daughter's debt. I had assumed that this money was available from an American-Jewish assistance organization to camp survivors, as a loan to be repaid when the party was in a position. But this was not the case. I made it clear that under no circumstances would I ask my 66-year-old, hard-working father with a very minimal income, to assume such a responsibility. I started working on other possibilities.

At the University of California at Berkeley, in February 1985, this question was put to me:

> *"You say that there was practically no merchandise*
> *in the stores or public services in Amsterdam when*

you arrived about six weeks after your liberation. How did you proceed, especially with your daughter?"

Our friends were very helpful in every way possible.

"We know that large sums of money were collected in the United States during the war to help survivors like you get a new start. Did you know anything about this? Were you ever approached? Did you realize that tremendous amounts of new clothing, bedding and household utensils were collected for you? Many of us worked very hard for those agencies, but you do not mention any of them."

I am sorry to disappoint you, but I received no help from any Jewish agency. I did not even know that this support was available; and if I had known, I am certain I would not have made use of the charity. Only one time was I forced to ask for help -- to purchase the boat tickets for my daughter and me to the United States, but without my father's guarantee on this "loan," the answer was, "Sorry!"

Siegfried's former employer was still paying me part of my husband's income. I imagined that he would be happy to hear I could relieve him of the responsibility of this agreement, if he would finance our trip. He was. We left Rotterdam on January 31, 1947, Doris very excited and I crying bitterly. We shared a cabin with two other women. Doris was seasick much of the time and I was so queasy that the most beautiful food I had seen in years did not appeal to me. After a stormy, uncomfortable crossing, we arrived, February 10, 1947.

I was recently asked,

"When did you finally accept the fact that your husband was not going to return, and how did you deal with it emotionally?"

I probably have never accepted that my husband, Siegfried, was killed by the Nazis. It is to be assumed that he and most of my closest friends are no longer alive, but accepting this as a fact is another matter. I could give no exact measurement of time, but at first I was convinced that he was alive, at some place under Russian protection. During the next period, I had to admit that he was never a physically strong person, overly sensitive in matters of bodily cleanliness and aesthetics. How could he really fight all that was expected to break each of us? On our last train trip he said to me, "I don't know where this journey will take us, but I don't think that I am capable of living through whatever it is. On the other hand, I am sure you will return to the normal life and to our child." Later on, during the last months in camp, I saw a similar loss of hope by my companions, which was always followed by a slow death. Siegfried, in his way, must have given up hope before the time.

Nr. LA.2952 TYPE: TB   UW Nr.

BIJLAGEN:

AMSTERDAM-C.,
STAALSTRAAT 7 b
TELEFOON 43066

Bij beantwoording
dagtekening en nummer
van deze brief vermelden

D E C L A R A T I O N.

The undersigned herewith declares that as appears from the Registers
of the Bureau, mentioned in the above head

Siegfried WOHLFARTH, born 26th March, 1904, at Homburg,

last address: Herculesstraat 3, Amsterdam

was deported - on the 3rd of September, 1944 - with destination Auschwitz (Poland).

Following documents, relating to this matter, are in the possession of
the undersigned:

A. Registercard of the former Joodse Raad (Jewish Council) in the name
   of Siegfried Wohlfarth, mentioned as above, mentioning that this
person came in the concentraion camp Westerbork (Netherlands) on the
29th of August, 1944 and marking the 3rd of September, 1944 as the date
of deportation;

B. A list, composed by or by the orders of the occupying power, called
   "Judentransporte aus den Niederlanden", dated 3rd September 1944, on
which list the personalia of Siegfried Wohlfarth, mentioned as above
figure - under No.745 - too.

Considering that since the deportation nothing was heard from or about
said person;
Further that on the whole deported persons immediately after their
arrival in the camp were killed by gas and after that cremated;
it may be ascertained that Siegfried Wohlfarth, mentioned as above,
on or about the 6th of September, 1944 lost his life by gas in or in
the surroundings of Auschwitz.

Amsterdam, 6th January 1947.

HET NEDERLANDSCHE ROODE KRUIS
the Chief of the Enquiry-Department:

S.Brookman.

The only declaration of Siegfried Wohlfarth's death.

PART IV:
1947 - 1979

With husband Robert.

After approximately 40 years in the United States, I look back to the day of my arrival and the first weeks following. I seem to have had a different experience than most newcomers. The fact that I did not want to come at all gave me a hopeless feeling when I saw the Statue of Liberty for the first time. I cried because I wanted the ship to go home; I was frightened, deadly afraid of this country and its unknowns. I knew so little about America, other than its discovery by Columbus and something vague about the Indians. Most of my knowledge came from books by Karl May, who himself had never been in America, but admired the "American Spirit." That spirit made it possible for you to find work if you really wanted it, live in any city you pleased, and work without a permit. Most important -- after five years I could apply for citizenship for Doris and me. I had studied English years before with little success. But I did not forget that my father and much of our family had come without any English, and much less formal education, and had found a home and a future.

We passed Ellis Island, and before arrival, the immigration control came on board to settle questions and arrange details. Doris and I had planned to stay a few days in New York, to see some relatives and old friends, so most of the baggage was sent by train to Chicago. It was wonderful to see familiar faces of our relatives, both Siegfried's and mine, but it was also strenuous, traveling alone by subway in a strange city without being able to speak the language.

While there, I accepted an invitation from Siegfried's cousin who had a resort hotel in the Catskills, to work there the first summer. Doris could come with me, since the hotel had a governess to care for the guests' children. I was assured that I could make good money, and I hoped this work would also bring me in contact with more people from those earlier years in Frankfurt. Perhaps this would lead to a more permanent job arrangement elsewhere.

We also visited Siegfried's only brother Hans, who then lived in New Jersey. He and his wife Alice had no children of their own, but had just adopted the two little girls of his wife's sister, who, with her husband, had not returned from deportation. There I was faced with the difficult task of telling Hans how his father had died quite suddenly after surgery in 1940, and the circumstances of his mother's suicide. Both of them, I reported, were buried at the Jewish cemetery close to Amsterdam.

We called on Siegfried's former employer at his office in New York to thank him for his assistance. He must have been concerned that we planned to stay in New York and again be a responsibility to him, for he looked relieved when I said we were heading for Chicago. He even suggested that I look for a job as a housekeeper, where I could keep my daughter with me. He gave Doris $50 and this was the last I ever heard of him.

We arrived in Chicago by train on a Sunday morning, having sat up all night, too excited to be tired. I had not seen my parents for more than seven years; Doris had been two when they left for the United States. They ordered a taxi and brought us to the new home they had found for us. It was nearly impossible to find living quarters so soon after the war; but they had found one good-sized furnished room, in a house quite close to their apartment. Not knowing what a rooming house was, I was shocked that we would share a bathroom with five or six other tenants! Doris and I had to sleep together in a Murphy Bed and the closet was in the common hallway. My parents had paid three months rent before I came, to be sure to have this place when we arrived. They had also had the place exterminated, they told me. I needed further explanation, for although I had had experience with all kinds of vermin, I had never seen roaches. Despite the extermination, they appeared shortly after we moved in.

On the afternoon of our arrival, many visitors came to my parents' small apartment. My cousin Martha's husband Julius had sponsored us, since my parents' income was not sufficient to secure the necessary guarantee. He offered me a job at a factory owned by one of his friends, but I had to reject his offer. My brother and his family lived in St. Louis and were expecting their second baby in early April. I wanted to plan my visit to St.

Louis to be of help to Eileen while she was in the hospital. Following that, I would begin my summer work at Fleischmann in the Catskills. Although Julius' friend would hire me unseen, and as much as I wanted and needed a regular job, there were two points I did not like. I could not expect a raise above my starting salary of $35 per week, and out of that I had to pay $18 a week for rent. I thanked my cousin very much for his kindnesses, but said I could not afford to accept his offer. He never forgave me.

Before leaving for St. Louis and New York, we rented a tiny room next to mine where Doris could sleep, and at last began to settle down. Doris was excited about everything she saw. I did not register her for school until fall, because of our travel.

We left early in April for our visit with my brother's family. Fred and I had not seen each other for 11 years. With 11 years difference in our ages, the political changes had affected us differently. When I got married, Fred was 13, and a short time later when we left for Holland, he was forced to quit school. He had spent three months in Buchenwald, until we secured his temporary visa to England, which insured his release from the concentration camp. Early in 1940, when he was 19 years old, he came to the United States with my parents, to join relatives in Chicago. They lived in a one-room apartment, with less than $50 among them. My father and mother spoke no English and my father was then 60 years old. We corresponded with them from Amsterdam until May 10, 1940, when Holland was occupied by the Germans and mail service was interrupted. Postal communication with the United States was established again somewhat later, but ceased in December 1941, following Pearl Harbor. My brother soon found a job in the book section of a department store, and he helped my father find work in the cafeteria. Their letter told of this fortunate employment and my father described his job thusly: "I am wearing a white uniform and a white cap and wheel a cart with dishes around the dining room." His salary was $8.00 per week. In our wildest imaginations, we could not understand what kind of occupations people had in the United States, but we were glad that they seemed settled. There had been no communication for two years, when suddenly it was announced that the International Red Cross would deliver messages into other countries, even into enemy territory. The letters could be no more than 20 words, which was difficult, but at least you could receive or send a sign of life.

My brother joined the American army and eventually my father advanced to a very good job as a waiter at a fancy private club. How he managed with his small vocabulary of English was something I never understood, but he loved his hard work. It was clear that my parents were happy in their new country.

We mailed our short note every month, and when we went into hiding, we used the name and address of Jo Vis. By my handwriting, they knew we were alive, but did not realize what this strange name and address meant. They wrote in 1943 that my brother, in the army but not yet overseas, had married during a furlough and that a little girl had been born. After our arrest in 1944, our communication was completely cut. My brother was shipped to Europe in the spring of 1945 and contacted our British relatives, Ena and Stanley, giving them the address on the Red Cross letters as a contact in Holland. Ena worked throughout the war to help refugees, especially Jewish children. She had the first contact with Doris because Jo Vis had returned from Dachau and could tell her where Doris was. A chaplain arrived from England to see what Doris needed and furnished her with a pair of badly needed shoes. He reported to Ena that we had been arrested and nothing was known about us.

At war's end, when Holland was occupied by the Canadians, Fred was in Germany with the American occupational forces, but he could never get permission to visit either Doris or me. I had seen him last when he was 16, in 1936, and we did not meet again until I arrived in April 1947, for our visit with his family in St. Louis.

Fred and Eileen had a small apartment in St. Louis, too small for their growing family, and Doris and I only compounded the space problem. We could barely communicate with my sister-in-law because of our language barrier, but nevertheless, we had a very good time. All went well, but the baby decided not to appear when expected. I had to leave St. Louis on April 29, to fulfill my commitment in New York, and the following night my nephew was born. Much later, in 1979 when I had retired to San Diego, it was Fred who was responsible for encouraging me to tell my story. I am sure that without him I never would have learned that young people are truly interested, even fascinated by what happened many years ago.

The resort hotel where I was to be employed was a large, beautiful development with exquisite German cuisine. One of the three couples who owned it were cousins of Siegfried. In advance of the summer season, which started on Memorial Day, everything had to be thoroughly cleaned, painted, and planted, including the buildings, cabins, the housing for the workers, the dining rooms, the kitchen and the bakery. It was an endless job, and bitter cold in the mountains. Doris and I shared a room in the women's dormitory, right under the slanting roof, which restricted sitting up in bed. She had the other children as company, I had food which was just heavenly, and everyone was very friendly. The relationship between the owners and workers was especially warm.

The first morning after breakfast, the work of the day was announced. My assignment was to clean all the bathrooms in the Annex, an old three-story building. At the end of the day, my lower back felt broken, but when I entered the dining room that evening, all eyes were on me. It took me some time before I realized that they were waiting for my complaints. I said nothing, took my seat and ate with a hearty appetite. Never again, in my five months there, did I get another assignment like that.

When the season opened, I was the waitress in the children's dining room, where I served three meals a day to about 75-100 children. It was wonderful work -- no babies, no feeding, just serving and supervising. My weekly salary was $35, including room and board for two. To supplement my income, I began working other jobs at the resort, and it became a busy seven-day week. But Doris had full days of real fun and excellent care. I became reacquainted with many people I had known in Frankfurt, all of whom were obviously doing well, because this resort was by no means inexpensive. My war experiences must have been known, for when people asked me about my future plans and I had to answer that I was looking for advice or work, the answer was usually the same, "I'm sure you will make it."

Many had lost close family members and had had difficulties getting into a secure country. Those people were quick to tell their stories, thinking I would understand because of my past. I appreciated what they were saying, but not only had I experienced the past with my own body and mind, I was deeply concerned about our future. Very soon I learned that the point of our conversations was to listen to their stories, and I stopped talking about myself completely, for years to come. By no means did I ever regret accepting this job. I learned a tremendous amount, and with the exception of English, German was the major language.

It was September 1947, before I returned to Chicago. I had spent two weeks with my parents at Fleischmann on their vacation, and while I continued working, I spent every minute I could spare with them. *Now* we had to begin a normal life. Doris, at first fluent only in Dutch, learned German through the contact with her grandparents and relatives, and now began to learn English. She was required to start school in the first grade, which was hard for a nine-year-old child. Children can be very cruel to foreigners, and Doris got her share. After six weeks, though, she was promoted to her grade and maintained very well.

It was time for me to look for work. I applied for many jobs and worked a short time at most. Either my knowledge of English was not sufficient, or I disliked the work. At one large company that I liked and where I thought, in time, I could advance, I was suddenly fired without explanation. Later I learned that this company never hired Jews. Apparently my strange accent hid this "dangerous" fact for a time. Anti-Semitism in this great melting pot -- what a disappointment for a greenhorn!

My mother reminded me that Edith, with whom I had gone to school, was also in Chicago. I contacted her and learned that she was living in a home for working mothers with children. The fact that the children were cared for when they returned from school sounded quite appealing to me, since I worried about Doris coming home, carrying her house key on a chain around her neck, entering this rooming house where so many different people lived. Edith invited me to look over her place. It was clean and well organized, but when I saw the facilities which had to be used by 20 or more adults and all their children, I found it even harder to take than our rooming house. I had lived too long with too many women, and could not accept this strict institutional atmosphere. The next day, our manager said she had a better combination of rooms for me if I were interested. It was $10 a week more, but I would have a large living room with a folding bed, a real kitchen, a porch and a small room for Doris. Optimistically, without a job, I accepted. I called Edith and told her my decision. She was also a widow, having lived for 10 years in Israel where her husband had died, and she had a daughter two years older than Doris. Edith worked in a department store, and I suggested that if something became available in my house, she might move in here. If that happened, we could share our evening meals, which would be more pleasant and home-like for both of us. She was interested.

My good friend Juro had given me a name and address of an old friend of his, who had immigrated to Chicago during the '30s, was married and had three children. At Juro's request, I called on his friend and we (Herman and Lillian) became good friends. Their oldest daughter, Doris, was the same age as mine and they had two more little girls. It was a wonderful, large family with Lillian's sisters and four brothers, and I was often a guest at their house. It was always warm and interesting to be with them. We discussed issues of all kinds, something I had missed for a long time. Not only did my English improve, but I began to acquire a knowledge of American life and culture. When I was fired from my job, I went to see Herman and Lillian. Her brother Harry was visiting, and although I did not know him too well, I told my short story. Harry consoled me, saying this was not the end of the world, and offered a solution. He and his brothers owned a chain of 150 stores nationwide, which sold inexpensive cotton dresses. He told me that it was not easy to get good managers for their stores and that if I accepted his offer, I would be trained in one of the largest stores, to take over a store in Chicago when I felt I was ready. During training, they could only pay me $35 a week, but I would make more when I became manager. I was surprised and afraid.

I had no knowledge of this kind of merchandise, and did not even understand the English to describe the materials being sold. Harry assured me that those were no problems, because I would learn all of this during the training period. I agreed.

The next morning I was at my assigned store, a very large place on a busy shopping street. The manager was a pleasant young woman and there were four or five sales girls. After I was shown around, she explained my duties as a manager of a store: not only must I keep my eyes on the floor and watch the sales help, I must learn the details of stocking and reordering. I was trained to trim the two huge windows once a week, and to watch the cashier. Once a week, inventory was taken, and missing merchandise or money was my responsibility. It was a lot to ingest, but I felt that I could handle what had to be done.

Since I had to work six days and two evenings weekly, (which changed after Thanksgiving to seven days and every evening), Doris had dinner with my mother, who stayed with her until she was asleep. My mother and Doris developed a very good relationship, and I was glad that they had this chance to be together. My father worked daily at lunch and dinner, so this arrangement worked well for them, too.

I was with The Cotton Shop for 11 years, commencing in 1948. For many years, I managed their largest store and was made to feel like a member of the family. Eventually Edith moved into our rooming house and started to work at the same company. When Doris and I finally moved to a decent apartment, Edith moved onto the same block. I learned how to drive and purchased a car. But when the company was sold, I moved on.

My attachment to my father was always very strong. Once, when I was perhaps 14, he told me how disappointed he had been that his first child was not a boy. But after he had had a son, everything was all right! Naturally I was hurt, but we were so close that I viewed the whole event rather humorously. After all, what could be done now? At 75 years old, my father was still working, and it was while he was *en route* to work at 7 a.m. in the year 1956 that he was killed by a hit-and-run driver.

That was also the year that Doris was married. Her husband

Doris at high school graduation, 1956.

Doris' husband Aharon.

Doris with her daughter Dannah in Israel, 1980.

had come from Israel to go to school in the United States. I, too, had been seeing eligible men, but none was interesting enough to pursue. I felt that my companion needed to have gone through similar experiences which, I thought, would have brought him to the same conclusions. I very much missed having someone with whom to discuss what was foremost on my mind. I had been intellectually dead since the Germans occupied Holland in 1940 and absolutely ignorant of what had happened in the other countries. My views of the war were one-sided, and based on much incorrect information. I started studying despite my shortage of time, and read first about the years in which I was most interested, about the countries on the "other" side: the United States, England, France, Russia, and the countries which had become involved in the war in ways similar to Holland. To increase my understanding of American history, I read translations of Upton Sinclair and Sinclair Lewis, as well as everything available about Roosevelt; but I did not understand the background fully until I had been here at least 10 years. British and French history to 1933 were very familiar to me, as was the earlier history of Russia. But I was obsessed with a desire to learn more.

I was truly lonely for someone with whom I could exchange ideas. Sometimes I discussed thoughts with my mother, who was at my house every Sunday since she was alone. She was disappointed that I did not want to accompany her to the synagogue, especially on the high holidays, but I never argued with her; I just didn't go. When Doris was younger, she had wanted to go to Sunday School at the synagogue, which was all right with me. I believe firmly in personal freedom of thought, of speech and decision, and never tried to influence my daughter to follow my beliefs. But when, one Sunday, my mother begged me again to go with her to services and at least fast on the high holiday of Yom Kippur, I explained that I would never fast again; that I had done all the fasting of my life. Never, ever did I want to feel hungry again. I tried to tell her what hunger really is and what it does to you. But I knew I had not reached her when she said suddenly, "I cannot understand why you always come back with those old stories. Forget those times and what has happened. Nobody wants to hear or talk about this anymore."

Since that time, 1957, many excellent works of scholars and reports by survivors have caused this part of history to be treated as fact. In the fall of 1985, the rabbi of the largest temple in town suggested that this should be the time for making the Holocaust a sacred event of the past; the time of mourning has to be over he said -- ENOUGH IS ENOUGH. There must have been more opposition to his suggestion than he expected; I am not informed as to how he is treating the subject today. One day of annual commemoration and a short review in Sunday School once or twice a year might be all the congregation wants to hear. There are painful memories awakened in any Jewish gathering where the Holocaust is a topic, but if we want our children and grandchildren to be informed of Jewish history, how can we overlook this period?

In April 1986, a Dutch writer, Harry Mulisch, spoke at the opening of the exhibition ANNE FRANK IN THE WORLD: 1929-1945, in Berlin, Germany. He said in part:

> "The fact that it (the Holocaust) did happen is the most persuasive deterrent for its ever happening again, just as the atom bombs that fell on Hiroshima and Nagasaki have probably prevented the Third World War thus far. We must continue to speak of the deaths of those millions of innocents till the end of time, not only to commemorate them but to prevent the death of further innocents. There is no better instrument than Auschwitz. And how about all those who keep complaining that it is time to stop talking about this war, because it happened forty years ago? They are the ones to keep an eye on. For first of all, the war did not happen all of forty years ago, but ONLY forty years ago. And besides, there was hardly any connection between the liquidation of the Jews and the war. The Second World War could have managed perfectly well without the Jewish Holocaust. The Holocaust was not an act of war, but something of a much darker nature -- a slaughter that was made possible by the chaotic circumstances of war, but was not necessarily a part of it.

> Except in Russia, people in Western Europe (and the United States) have mostly stopped talking about that war. Who here still mentions the invasion, or the Battle of the Bulge? No, we speak of Auschwitz, Treblinka and maybe Maidanek, not battlefields but places for which there are no other names than Auschwitz. We can learn nothing about Auschwitz by calling it hell, but should we want to find out about hell, then Auschwitz is the place to study."

My personal life was undergoing some permanent changes, and I needed legal advice. An attorney was recommended, and I made an appointment at his office. The professional part was completed to my satisfaction. The man was respectful and intelligent, but for some reason I wished he were less aloof. I knew nothing about him and I was curious. The year was 1955. Ten years had passed since the end of the war, and I was 46.

My interest in the attorney grew; but he did not get in touch with me. There was only one thing to do, something I had never done in my life. I invented a legal question and called him at his office. We discussed my query and I stretched the conversation into a variety of other subjects. Obviously he enjoyed the talk, for he asked if we could continue the discussion, perhaps at dinner two nights later. This was the beginning of a happy relationship, each of us matured under different and difficult circumstances. Our backgrounds were as different as could be, but our ethical values and religious convictions were very much the same. He had a thorough knowledge of history and a magnificent memory. I was surprised at his knowledge of European history and the intensity with which he had followed the war years on every front.

Robert Waterford was divorced and lived with his two sons. I lived alone after Doris' marriage, and my mother was suggesting that she and I move together into a large apartment. Our expenses would be less and it would be nice for me to come home to a prepared dinner. It seemed very logical for her, but I did not want to give up the freedom and independence I had learned to appreciate for the first time in my life. My

FACES OF THE RIGHTEOUS GENTILES

Ab Reusink

Rinus Hille

Gre Driessen

Joe Vis, 1946

Joe Vis, 1986

mother and I had not agreed on too many issues since my early years, and I did not want to live in constant fear of arguments. Neither did Mother approve of my developing association with Robert, and I certainly did not want daily discussions about this relationship that had become so valuable to me. Her fear of sharing me was understandable, now that she was alone after a long marriage. That I had been widowed at 36 and I had managed this lonely life and the responsibilities for more than 10 years, was hard for her to understand, because I never complained. Now that her life was lonely, she was fearful. Because I understood her feelings so well, it was even harder for me to deny my mother such an understandable request. I found it very difficult to explain my decision to her.

Two years later, after returning from a disappointing trip to Germany where she had sought out old friends, Mother had a heart attack. She told her sister that I had broken her heart. She was quite ill, and had a second attack while still in the hospital. When she came home, I hired a woman to stay with her and she recovered slowly.

In August of 1958, two years after Doris' wedding, Robert and I married. Doris lived in a new high rise apartment complex close to Lake Michigan, and we moved nearby. Early the following year I changed careers. The clothing stores were sold to an indifferent group and the hours were becoming too long. A challenging career was now more important to me than the income. Through some friends on the staff, I was fortunate to find an interesting new job in a large hospital close to our home. I was trained as a clinic coordinator in the outpatient ward. After five years of talking with hundreds of patients and learning basic medical routines, I came in contact with a research group from the University of Illinois, where I had the opportunity to be trained as a medical technician for a cardiovascular research program which was trying to determine under what conditions strokes happen or recur. I worked for the University until transferring to the Chicago Heart Association, which had taken over our entire team. There I stayed until retiring (I thought) in 1971.

During those years, it seemed impossible to find anyone in the entire city of Chicago who was at all interested in that recent history that had so drastically shaped all our lives. I knew where I *could* find these people, though; and I wanted to share this period of my life with Robert, so we returned to Europe in 1961, the same year my mother died.

It was a nostalgic return. We began in Amsterdam, where I had many old friends -- survivors and our Gentile supporters. Ab Reusink and the De Boers had died. Gre Driessen had not changed a bit, still a loving, warm friend. The Tjeertes family was much larger. Rinus had married and Jo Vis, my old, reliable friend was still there. Trude and Richard Joseph, she the sister of my closest friend Irene, had two teenage daughters and lived in a beautiful house, not far from Den Haag, the capital of Holland. My friend Juro had remarried and also had two daughters. We all had maintained correspondence, but it was so good to meet personally again.

It was extremely difficult for me to go to Amsterdam, where I had spent my happiest and my saddest years. Rarely through-out my life have I lost control of my emotions, but visiting the Hercules Straat nearly broke me. I felt sorry for Robert on this day, but he understood very well. The events of the war that my Dutch friends and I experienced have left unbreakable ties. Our supporters were honored as Righteous Gentiles at Yad Vashem, the museum and teaching institution of the Holocaust, for having saved so many lives, Doris' and mine among them.

In 1980, at Brigham Young University in Utah, shortly before I teamed with Alfons Heck, I was asked a question that took a little time to answer.

> *"How did your faith influence you in your hardest times?"*

> What the young woman and the large aud-ience expected to hear, I was sure, was the least complicated and most obvious answer. But it was a serious, sincere question which deserved an honest answer, for which I had to go far back. into my youth as an assimilated and secular Jew in Germany. My life style and education were very different from orthodox Jewish family life. Very early I had learned to understand which

ethical values are necessary to be a strong and
independent person. This was and is my faith. As
a very young woman, during the most difficult
time of my life, as close to death as anyone can
come, I depended on myself, and will continue to
do so, as long my body supports me.

Robert and I left Amsterdam for Prague, Czechoslovakia,
where we wanted to visit the site of the camp at Kratzau in the
Sudeten. We were anxious, also, to get a visa and permission to
visit Auschwitz in Poland. The permission and visa were not
granted, so Auschwitz was off the itinerary. But we succeeded in
getting to Reichenberg, which had train connections to Kratzau.
Our arrival in Kratzau was quite unremarkable; it was greatly
changed. The German families had had to leave so the Czechs
could return. It seemed lifeless. The butcher shop I remembered
so clearly was still there, but probably under different ownership. The factory had been returned to its owners and on the
roof was a red neon star. I asked the person at the gate if he by
any chance knew about the women's camp which had been in
Paradise Valley during the war. He remembered and gave me
quite valuable information.

A local woman, who knew all about the graves in the
cemetery, answered questions about where our women were
buried. The woman knew that the graves existed, but naturally
there were no names. We had no chance of getting there, for if
we missed our train to Reichenberg, this village had no hotel to
host foreigners.

I found the route we had taken daily to the camp and we
walked slowly through beautiful Paradise Valley. Every step
seemed familiar to me and many memories, mostly painful
ones, returned. There is a creek running though this valley and I
recalled one day when we were on our way home from work in
the early morning, hearing a woman call for help. To our
surprise we saw the commandant, a woman about 40 years old,
fully clothed in the creek. Her hands clutched the bank, but she
could not get a good hold, and was afraid she would be carried
away by the water. My first and meanest instinct was to step on
her fingers -- avenging came quickly in our situation, even to the
strongest pacifist's mind. But some of our women did come to

her aid, and I must admit I did not like this. What had gotten this woman into this situation at 6:30 a.m.? There were many rumors: she had tried to kill herself over problems with her superiors, she had discovered an unfaithful lesbian friend.... Unfortunately we never learned the truth; she was gone the same day.

There was an enormous tree to which we had to run during air raid warnings, and those were some of our happiest moments at Kratzau. Unfortunately, the airplanes always flew on. As illogical as it sounds, a bomb would have proved to us that somebody knew where we were. I recalled the daily walks, especially in winter, with lots of snow and smooth, hard ice. Many of us had no shoes, only rags tied together with other rags. Nobody had stockings of any kind, so frostbite on feet and legs was nothing unusual. Our medical team was not equipped to treat conditions which required anything more than aspirin or a dressing made out of paper. The male guards who alternated with the females in accompanying us to and from work, sometimes carried thin branches and enjoyed switching our naked legs. It hurt, but did not make us walk faster.

After a time, Robert and I came out of the woods into a clearing, and there stood the stone building where we had been housed. At first it looked just as I remembered it, but coming closer into the court where we had stood so many hours at roll call regardless of weather, staring for endless weeks at the kitchen window frame where we awaited our skimpy meals, I noticed that the building was sagging. Entering the doorway, I saw the ceilings of the upper floors rotting and bending in the middle. Suddenly I moved my hand to my neck, searching for something that was not there. Subconsciously I was reacting as I had daily, more than 16 years ago, clutching at my neck for the WERK KRATZAU pin that closed the top of my dress to protect against the cold.

As mentioned, it was of utmost importance to locate a piece of string to use as a belt, to stop the cold air from blowing against your skin. For the last five or six months I hung on this "belt" a reddish enamel drinking cup, very worthwhile for all kinds of unusual experiences apart from drinking. At Auschwitz for example, when we were not allowed to leave the barrack to go to the latrine, and later at Kratzau, when the latrines were in such unspeakable condition, we had to utilize our cups for urination. My tattered, rusty cup now hangs above my cooking range, never evoking a curious question from visitors but greeted lovingly by me every day.

With some reluctance, we ventured inside the remains of the camp. There, still visible on the walls, were Germans instructions regulating the conduct of prisoners and guards. Otherwise, there was only straw, debris and filth. Nothing had been done since we left; the building was dying and I was standing there, alive and well! I never did or will feel as victorious and strong as I did this day in Kratzau.

As I stood within the crumbling building, I flashed back to my work at an electrical bench, one of several standing in long rows, all facing the same direction. To my right had been another row of different machines, the noise and humming of which became very routine. We worked from 6 a.m. until 12 noon, when there was a signal for a 30-minute interruption, and all machines were quiet. After a short pause to go to the primitive toilet, one still had 20 minutes left to relax. We had nothing to eat during this time, and there were no chairs on which to sit, so I remember finding a place to sit on the floor and rest my back on the wall. We started again at half past noon, and worked until 6 p.m. when our guards marched us home to the camp for the evening meal.

While servicing my machine, I always sang. Nobody could hear over the noise of the machines and my voice was never anything to be proud of, but I enjoyed singing all those German songs from years and years ago. Happy *volks* songs, parts of operas, popular songs from my youth, ballads, anything. Very often on those occasions, I felt a light tapping on my right upper back close to the shoulder. I would turn, expecting to find somebody ready to issue an order. Sometimes I was sure that Siegfried would be standing there to surprise me; it was like an hallucination, but never disappointing. When entering the camp grounds on my 1961 visit, I suddenly felt that tapping I had experienced so often but, had until now, forgotten.... It happened only one time; never again.

We returned to Reichenberg by train and spent some days in the beautiful city of Prague. Seeing the former Jewish quarters which date to the early Middle Ages, the cemeteries and synagogues, some of them built in the 11th century, and knowing that so much of this had been destroyed, as well as the lives of nearly 80,000 Jews, gave our trip the crowning sentiment.

We were taken to a synagogue which was no longer in use. Although completely empty, the walls in each of the few rooms told the story, where words failed. Every wall was covered with names, birth and death years of each person deported from Prague to Auschwitz, always via Theresienstadt. There were special lights that could be directed to each name, so visitors might look for their relatives or friends. When we returned to Prague in 1975, this synagogue had been closed and has never been opened since. I have in my workroom a small photo of one of those walls. While I don't need it as a reminder, this picture serves as a daily inspiration.

PART V:
1979 - Present

Alfons Heck and Helen Waterford.

I continued working for the Chicago Heart Association for ten years. During that time, Doris' family moved to St. Louis, where my two grandchildren were born. After she and her husband Aharon had attained advanced educational degrees, they moved to Israel, Aharon's homeland. Having my only child so far away was, and still is, hard to take. Robert and I made several trips to Israel in the intervening years, and when the travel became too strenuous, Doris began coming to visit us annually.

Robert had been talking about spending the cold winters away from Chicago, and by 1972, we were ready to try another place. After investigating many possibilities, we decided on San Diego. For Robert it was not an easy decision, retiring and changing a long time residence together. I had no preference as to whether we stayed in Chicago or moved to a milder climate. Because my roots were not planted as deeply, I was able to pick up and go where Robert wished. As it happened, it was in San Diego where I began the work that I now find so fulfilling.

It was February 1979, the time of year when the bitter winter weather brings many visitors to mild San Diego. My brother Fred, freezing in St. Louis, comes yearly around this time to thaw out. Our relationship is close, and we share a great interest in the history of the Holocaust.

This time, a few days into his visit, Fred suddenly asked, "Would you like to join me in teaching a three-week Holocaust course?" Without asking how, where or when, I agreed unconditionally. I knew now what I had been waiting to do; I simply had not known how. For more than 30 years, I had talked little about my experiences except to Robert, knowing that most people would rather forget those unfortunate years of 1933-1945.

It seems that Michelle, my brother's oldest daughter, was living in Fairbanks, Alaska. She and her husband were associated with the university, and it had been her idea to suggest her father as the teacher for this summer program. When he was accepted, he must have had second thoughts, being just as inexperienced in public speaking as I. So as not to feel quite so alone in this venture, he asked me to come along. It would be in July of 1979.

What I needed, besides an outline for our combined undertaking, was to find some groups willing to listen to me, to make me feel easier when facing an audience. I started a campaign of telephone calls to synagogues, Jewish organizations, churches, clubs and well-known civic groups, offering at no charge, my knowledge and experiences from the Holocaust period in the form of lectures, courses, or discussions. Sad to say, I was not very successful after weeks on the telephone. I remember Robert saying to me, "In my opinion, you are humiliating yourself with your offers; I would never be able to go that far."

Those thoughts had never come to mind. I was deeply motivated to share what I had to offer, because I have a responsibility as a witness to do what I am able, to insure that the crimes of bigotry and racial prejudice not be forgotten. In truth I did find some attentive listeners, even two or three actual dates, but in proportion to my efforts, it seemed very little.

A day has been chosen annually for the past 8-10 years, to remember the Holocaust internationally. In Hebrew, it is called *Shoah* -- Destruction. The date was selected to commemorate the beginning of the uprising in the Warsaw Ghetto, in April of 1943. This was the day that the Germans had intended to clear the last 70,000 Jews out of the ghetto and ship them by train to the extermination camps. The date is set after the Jewish calendar, which makes it a different date every year on the Roman calendar. In 1979, it was April 23 and 24. I attended my first Holocaust Seminar at the University of San Diego and, for the first time, heard a survivor speak. It was enormously interesting, and very helpful in preparing me for my own lectures in July. I found that my knowledge, gathered over many years of experience and reading, could stand up to addresses of both academic and lay speakers. The woman's manner of presentation was not to my liking; not so much the subject matter, but the way in which she used a pitiful, whining approach to awaken compassion in her audience. She spoke not more than 25 minutes, but many people were silently crying. It was clear to me that I could not lecture in this format. As little as I knew about the professional presentation of ideas to an audience, I followed my common sense. If the listener gets emotionally involved, I decided, if pity is aroused (which is by no means the same as empathy), if the handkerchiefs appear, then the thinking process stops. At that point, I do not have the complete attention of the audience, and cannot explain the real reasons that I am there to speak to them. I let my listeners take part in my personal life, which is not always pretty, but they know that every word is true. Sometimes I inject a little humor to ease the intake of such serious matter. I am a cheerful person who is fortunate to be able to see the best in nearly everything. With this approach, my listeners feel personally involved and can relate to my story, even though they are of my grand-children's generation. For them, a new world opens.

It was at this Holocaust seminar that I learned of the Jewish Agency which had created a speakers bureau for Jewish topics, including the Holocaust. I offered my services the following day. Immediately I was sent to high schools, junior highs, churches and workshops of the San Diego Public Schools. The agency received high praise about my visits from every place I spoke. The youngsters in my audiences relived my experiences with me, and the final 15 minutes that I reserved for questions was never long enough. Everyone was satisfied with my work and I was glad to be on the right track. I felt ready for Alaska.

Fred and I discussed our program in detail. He was acquiring some excellent movies and documentaries, and we planned our agenda carefully. My brother's primary interest is in the history of anti-Semitism, and in academic Holocaust research. To complement his expertise, I am very well-informed on the treatment of the Jews in nearly every occupied country of Europe, and the personal experiences of many, many victims.

As a result of my speaking engagements in San Diego I knew that I did not need written notes; the material was imprinted in my mind. Fred was scheduled to begin the first and second evenings (about three hours each) with a history of anti-Semitism and he chose the Middle Ages as his starting point. It never occurred to me that Fred might suffer from stage fright; I was looking forward excitedly to speaking! Only much later did Fred admit that he had had this problem. We very much enjoyed presenting the course, and for the last session, asked the students to prepare a paper explaining why they had wanted to participate in the program, what they had found most and least interesting, and what they had learned from the presentation. In general, they seemed to appreciate the different points of view, and the very personal approach. As we prepared to leave Fairbanks, Esther, my sister-in-law, struck up a conversation with a woman named Camille who lived in Anchorage and taught at the University of Alaska. She was originally from St. Louis, and it developed that her major in college had been the Holocaust. What made this disclosure even more unusual was the fact that she was Black. When we asked how she had become interested in this field, she replied that she and her brother had been adopted by a Jewish couple as children. The couple were survivors of the Holocaust, had not been able to have children, and had raised their adopted family in the Jewish faith. Mostly to honor those loving people, she had decided to make the Holocaust her field of study. My brother had to leave the next day, but I went on to Anchorage with Camille, who showed me around the city and invited me to her home. On subsequent visits to Anchorage, I have tried to contact Camille, but cannot locate her.

When schools reopened in the fall, many speaking engagements came my way, not only in San Diego but at universities in Arizona, Utah and the state of Washington. One day I read an article in the local paper by a man writing about his life in the Hitler Youth. I had no particular plan in mind when I tried to contact Alfons Heck. My first reaction was curiosity. To publicly and voluntarily write about his past, showed clearly that he was different from his German contemporaries. On my return visits to Europe, East Germans always maintained that there had been very few Nazis in their part of Germany. West Germans, with two exceptions, denied ever having belonged to the Hitler Youth, even though it was mandatory for children over 10 years of age.

Our first phone conversation was somewhat halting on both

sides. After giving Alfons my name, background, and interest in speaking about my experiences in the San Diego vicinity, there was a long moment of silence. I did not realize how surprised he was to get a call from a Jewish survivor. He could not guess what this woman wanted from him! Suddenly my plan took form; I asked him if he would be willing to participate in this Jewish speakers bureau, and speak to schools about *his* experiences. So little was known about these children soldiers that I assumed (incorrectly) that everybody would be as curious as I.

Alfons accepted my invitation to a meeting of the speakers bureau, consisting of other speakers and some community leaders. The outcome of this gathering was a total surprise to both of us, but it showed clearly that hate and vengeance are so close to the surface that most people are ready to attack without even wanting to learn or listen. The other speakers were cool, actually hostile to Alfons. It was all my fault; I was ignorant and quite naive. I had assumed that everyone was speaking about the Holocaust in the hope that those years, those crimes and experiences would never be forgotten. I felt that we needed to study, learn and try to understand that perhaps not all Germans had been involved in the crimes of the Nazi party. We needed to comprehend that there were Germans who were accepting a common burden of guilt for the atrocities of the period.

When Alfons Heck and I first spoke together in 1980, shortly after our presentation to the speakers bureau, we were an unexpected success. The San Diego teachers to whom we spoke were fascinated, and it took more than four hours to answer their countless questions. Soon we were contacted by *Good Morning America*; it seemed we were on our way! Shortly after this engagement, the Jewish speakers bureau asked for another meeting. There, I was reprimanded for speaking with "the Nazi." Those in attendance were told of our appearance on *Good Morning America*, where I had related my empathy for Nazi orphans after the war, proving, they asserted, how dangerous I must be for their cause. Obviously, I had to reassess my speaking engagements, to allow myself to be free of any obligations to this agency. I was determined that my future speeches, with or without Mr. Heck, would not depend upon permission from this or any other agency. I would be available if they ever wanted me, but under no condition would I give up my freedom to speak with whomever I chose. Until then, I had not comprehended how difficult it is to eradicate prejudice.

I needed to remember my goal: that the years 1933-1945 never, never be forgotten. Jews especially, should not have to be reminded; we are supposed to know. It is so we may remain constantly aware, that we observe the annual day of remembrance. My memories are with me 24 hours a day. I will never forget what has happened, nor should anyone else. But at the same time, I will carry no excess luggage like hate or revenge. Speaking to varied groups is one very important way to come closer to our goal.

In early 1981, following an article in the Los Angeles *Times*, Alfons and I began receiving invitations to speak together locally. I was excited, because our reception was generally very satisfactory. Meanwhile, our friends in San Diego felt that it was unfair that I was speaking only to strangers, while they knew so little about my past. I was still quite reserved when discussing my life with relatives, friends or acquaintances, having felt too often how little they were truly interested. But I could not resist this invitation. They arranged a gathering of 25 or 30 people, all quite close friends. I described my life between 1933 and 1945, and they were with me fully, especially during the painful years of separation from our child and the joy of our eventual reunion. I talked about the period following, when I had felt stifled in mentioning the war years.

Subsequently I told of my desire to understand the perpetrators of this horror, explaining that it was clear that a new communication base must be created if we wished to live in a peaceful world. I told the group about my speaking partner, about his past and current values, but that was when the mood of the gathering changed. They absolutely would not believe that I did not hate all Germans, particularly since I had felt their power first hand. What could be gained by denying hatred, they wanted to know? I had learned only too well that hate is a boomerang which only destroys the sender, I told them. I wanted to build peace, not feed the flame of continuous destruction. It had become clear to me that each generation

Helen Waterford, lecturing independently, and below, with former Nazi Alfons Heck, throughout the 1980s.

must be flexible, ready for change and the necessary adjustments.

At that point, a rather basic realization struck me: How can one predict how he will react if his information is based on hearsay rather than personal experience? These people had never been in my shoes or at the places I discussed, yet they harbored such hatred that they were disappointed in me and my reactions. There was little to do but thank them for organizing this gathering and listening to stories far removed from their lives. But I was quite disappointed that nobody could understand that young people, such as many of the Hitler Youth, often see their lives differently from an adult perspective, and that all of us are entitled to seek redemption for events caused by our ignorance and immaturity.

Al had been threatened verbally by Neo-Nazis after stating his position in various articles. These threats came from a side I had not expected, and I, too, was not overlooked in their ugly behavior. Survivors also attended some of our presentations, especially to air their hate. Older survivors who, since 1945, had never seen another Nazi, found here a man honest enough to admit membership in the Hitler Youth, saying he was once proud to have belonged. They reacted like bulls attacking the red cloth. Blindly aggressive against both of us, they became more and more agitated as they talked, and our host group did little to discourage them. Later, I became more upset than Al and blamed myself that I had involved him in what were becoming very unpleasant situations.

Then suddenly it happened against me -- after more than five years of combined lectures, when our presentations had become so popular that universities often had to wait many months before scheduling us. I was confronted early in 1986 at a well-known university in upstate New York. Hate exploded, noisy and mean. Naturally I was aware that hate existed against me in certain groups -- I realized after many years of trying to bridge the gap, that I was battling deep and seemingly terminal prejudice. But I felt helpless when a group of 10-12 young Jewish students began yelling remarks that made my life, my hopes and successes seem to collapse like a house of cards. They

tried to overwhelm me with their undisciplined, often unin-
telligible screaming -- throwing out questions, disregarding who
had the floor. The youngsters in this large audience seemed
unable to distinguish their hate against the Germans who brutal-
ized, tortured or perhaps killed their grandparents, from hatred
against second or third generation Germans who were in no way
responsible for the sins of their ancestors. How long will we
carry this vengeance? Will we continue to hate into infinity?

While we will forever mourn, revenge must never detract
from remembering our dead. To condemn *all* Germans reduces
us to the level of the Nazis, who hated every Jew, every gypsy,
every Slav. Although I repeat myself, it cannot be said often
enough: if we follow the scripture, 'an eye for an eye'... we all
will eventually be blind.

Strangely enough, the basis of the students' complaints
against me was my way of reporting my experiences during
1944-1945. They rejected my description of the train ride from
Holland to Auschwitz, the three selections by Dr. Mengele, the
weeks without food or water, with no undergarments or shoes
during the winter, as "an interesting, but colorless and harmless
history lesson." They wanted to hear what the Germans had
done to me, physically and explicitly. My answer -- that in my
years of speaking, I have intentionally refrained from describing
gory and bloody events -- was not accepted. Nevertheless, I will
continue to refrain from the sensational, because I feel it is
immoral to get explicit, simply to awaken emotions and sensa-
tions in my audiences.

At the end, I told the students that in more than five years of
lecturing, Mr. Heck and I had naturally had listeners who did
not agree with our presentation -- this is their right -- but never
had we been the victims of such massive, undisciplined aggressive chaos. They constantly interrupted each other, with com-
ments like 'What kind of a Jew are you?' and 'You should be
ashamed!' At last, policemen who had watched outside the
entrance door started to walk inside very slowly, and gradually
order returned to the audience. I reminded the students that
they had called me a person without courage, saying that I was
too cowardly to tell my experiences truthfully. And then I ended
this encounter with the words, "I don't think that I deserve this."

That brought many, many listeners to rousing applause and a standing ovation. ·

Despite our treatment, I wondered, "Why do I feel only embarrassment for these badly mannered, ignorant Jewish children?" But on second thought I realized it was not just embarrassment, it was deep sadness that I felt. I speak to every group about prejudice, the evil root of genocide. I may often change my wordings or examples but never my major theme, that hating a people and wanting them to die only perpetuates the unbelievable crimes of earlier generations. Hating a people from previous generations, most of whom are personally unknown, is not only self-destructive, but can destroy this whole generation.

We lecture at schools all over the country. Some months we leave home early Monday morning and return Friday night. For me, it is a dream come true. I have been asked, 'What is your purpose in maintaining such an exhausting schedule at your age, speaking about an event that started more than 50 years ago?'

As different as are Alfons Heck's and my backgrounds, our experiences and particularly our ages, and despite the fact that we disagree on many issues, we do have one common goal. We have found that by our unique combination and our manner of presentation (taking turns in chronological order), that our audiences understand our purpose and the history of our subject. We believe that ignoring or pretending that the events of the Holocaust did not occur makes a repetition of this shameful period more likely.

At every presentation Al and I are asked how we met and how we are getting along. Our listeners are also curious about our private lives. Sometimes I am asked when I stopped hating Mr. Heck, it being assumed that I must have hated him, as I would hate any former Nazi. Despite their assurance that they understand _why_ we are speaking, they have difficulty with my explanation, that I have never felt what is commonly referred to as hate. We could not accomplish our goal of making others understand the impact of this period of history if there were hate or even dislike between us. To keep history's memories alive, instead of erasing the past, I have had to change no feelings regarding Mr. Heck.

I recently conducted a six-week course about the Holocaust, for a group of San Diego school teachers and other interested adults, arranged by the school district. The last evening was set aside for reporting my personal tribulations and some postwar conclusions. The question "Why the Jews"? surfaced many times.

I replied quite honestly that I could not give a satisfactory answer, that the answer was speculative, even for the wisest of men. An older man in the audience, an observant student who never missed a class, told me excitedly that he knew exactly why this persecution and genocide had been directed at the Jews. Said he, "You are a German Jew. You must be familiar with the fact that the Jews of Germany only wanted to be Germans and did not accept God anymore. This was the punishment for all Jews for the disloyalty of the German Jews."

The man was quite serious, so I answered him in the same manner. "The Jews are distributed in many countries. In every country they show their loyalty the same way as Christians: First, one is a citizen of one's country and second, a member of his religious group. So felt every German Jew before 1933. If your conclusion as to punishment is correct, I wish you would explain why more than three million Polish Jews, whose closer ties to their religion is well-known, were murdered like any other Jews."

Anti-Semitism is very popular with people who favor the death penalty or in a population where there are strong prejudices on religious or racial issues, (a society which harbors hate against those who are somehow different). War is an excellent camouflage for genocide. These conclusions have brought me closer to the conviction that hating and looking for revenge with which to teach the "enemy" a lesson, are the emotions that prevent understanding and communication.

Monuments at the Ravensbrueck Concentration Camp for women, located in East Germany.

Jewish cemetery in Frankfurt am Main, showing evidence of anti-Semitic actions today.

Jo Vis, center, is honored as a Righteous Gentile at Yad-Vashem in Jerusalem. To his right is Doris.

Piet and Gre Tjeertes are honored at a similar ceremony in Den Haag, Holland.

Robert and Helen Waterford, 1985.

PART VI:
Epilogue

May 1986

The city of Frankfurt am Main tried, for many years, to maintain contact with its former Jewish citizens who had been forced to leave during 1933-1945. All new books published about historical Frankfurt, the Frankfurt we knew, as well as those about the destruction during the war and the complete rebuilding are mailed to us yearly. They offer beautiful but painful memories. The six-story building with shops, offices, and apartments on the fifth floor, where I lived with my parents and brother, was pictured in one of the books. It shows it as it looked when we lived there, and when I left after marriage. Another photo shows the house after a heavy bombardment, and a final photo shows an office building on the same space, modern and completely impersonal.

The city has also developed a plan to show former 'Frankfurters' the city of today and try "in this small way" (as they put it) to bring those earlier years alive again. Every year, a group of older Jews, former citizens, is invited to visit the city. The annual participants are selected by the city staff according to age, meaning the oldest were invited first. Naturally over the years, applicants were eliminated by illness, death or other complications. My turn came in 1986. Robert and I were invited to spend two weeks in May in Frankfurt, all expenses paid. The group was large -- about 120 people from all over the world -- Australia, South America, South Africa, Israel and the United States. The program our hosts had planned included city tours to view the unbelievable changes in our hometown, as some of us had been gone more than 50 years. We saw where the aged and ill Jewish survivors were housed. There was a bus tour to the city of Worms, where the first Jewish settlers had come with the Romans when they conquered central Europe nearly 2000 years ago. Worms is also the city where, in 1521, Martin Luther was condemned as a heretic. Outside Frankfurt are forts dating from Roman times. We had a boat trip on the river Main, a part of the city which played an important roll in every child's life. An opera visit and two receptions at the more than 1000-year-old city hall were included. Civil marriage ceremonies are still performed here, as was mine in 1933. The hotel where we stayed for two weeks was the city's oldest and most elegant, the FRANKFURTER HOF, a place few of us had seen from the inside while we lived in the city. Our public transportation, too, was free.

It is difficult for the old-timer to find remembrances of the past or even find his way in the new Frankfurt. The street where I grew up had disappeared, and the large closed in market for produce and meats with it. This centuries-old ghetto where the Rothschilds were born, housed the two largest synagogues, until the crystal night of 1938. When the rubble was being removed from those narrow streets, an old Roman wall was discovered not too far underground. Reconstruction in this area was stopped for several years, to decide what to do about this ancient wall.

As early as the twelfth century, Frankfurt had been a small but well-organized community. In 1241 the Jewish houses were demolished and more than three-quarters of the population was massacred. Ultimately the city was granted a royal pardon and the safety of the Frankfurt Jews was guaranteed. In 1349, in the surge of hatred aroused by the Black Death, the entire community was wiped out, along with most other Jewish communities in Germany. In the fifteenth century, the Jews were enclosed by walls and gates in a ghetto, after demands by the emperor and the Catholic church, including the Pope himself.

Frankfurt had become a center of Jewish learning and commercial and social enterprise, but the Jews were again expelled from the city in 1614, after an open rebellion by the rabble. Two years later, Jews were ceremoniously returned to the ghetto, with terms designed to keep their numbers stationary, allowing a maximum of 500 families and 12 marriage licenses annually. In 1811 the ghetto was finally abolished, by orders of Napoleon, and a declaration of equal rights for all citizens expressly included the Jews.

Nazi actions against the Jews began on April 1, 1933, with a
boycott, followed on April 7 by the dismissal of Jewish white-
collar workers, university teachers, actors and musicians. At this
time about 30,000 Jews lived in Frankfurt; by September 1943,
Frankfurt's Jewish population totalled 500, including half-Jews.
We had left Frankfurt in 1934 amid a confusing mix of feelings.
Leaving all of our relatives to an unknown but obviously
dangerous future, completely overpowered the relief of escaping
into freedom.

Returning in 1986 brought back many days of my childhood,
but it did not depress me or make me pine for former days. I
loved this city, appreciated its cultural offerings and excellent
schooling; but there is no one now living in Frankfurt whom I
knew from former years -- nobody and nothing to come home
to.

In our group were two people I did know. One was Edith, my
former schoolmate whom I found again in Chicago and have
been close to ever since. The second was a man I never would
have recognized had I not seen his last name on the nameplate
of a woman. I asked her if her husband, by chance, was named
Ernst. He was standing next to her, and I thought he looked
somewhat familiar, but we had not seen each other since 1926.
Suddenly I said to Robert, "Would you like to meet the man who
broke my heart when I was 17?" Ernst and I looked at each
other (60 years is a very long time) and we remembered. He had
left Frankfurt when he was 21 to accept a job in Duesseldorf; we
had been friends for some months before, and I had cried my
heart out when he left. He and his wife were now living in New
York.

Despite the fact that at least half the people in our group
were former Frankfurters, strangely they remembered very
little. Some of them hardly knew what schools they had
attended. To me it seemed that they had tried and succeeded in
erasing their pasts, because adjustment in their new homes had
been difficult. Only one other person had been in a camp during
the war and he absolutely did not want to talk about it. All the
other people had left Germany around 1938, had learned a new
language and settled down in their new homes.

Many of the European Jews adjusted to their new environments by trying to forget the painful past. Their difficult years are buried deeply, practically as a period of shame. Losses of family, friends, property, social and professional standing differed, depending on location and the time of occupation by Germany. But these people shared one common emotion: a blatant hate of all Germans and anything connected with Germany, despite the fact that they had just accepted this generous trip. As many times as I have encountered this phenomenon, it always surprises me. A short time ago, I talked to an old school friend who lives in New York, knows my past and my lecture work. She said that none of her friends, who probably also know me from earlier years in Europe, ever want to talk to me. "Why?" I asked, astonished. "Because you care so much for the Germans and you visit Germany all the time." She also mentioned my lectures with this former Nazi, which proved that I must love "Them", instead of sharing a common hatred.

After our two interesting weeks in Frankfurt, Robert and I planned to visit Luxembourg. Doris arrived from Tel Aviv to meet us, and we drove to the northernmost part of this miniature country, to a small town with a lovely hotel. A large marker in the front garden advises the visitor that an American 12th Regiment unit stayed here in December 1944, during the Battle of the Bulge. Here at the Parc Hotel in Berdorf, about 60 men were stationed, one of five companies battling the sudden, successful assault by the German army. The order came for all five companies *not* to retreat, and all could be reached but the Berdorf unit. Five tanks with riflemen were sent to Berdorf as a relief force, but the crew mistook the Parc Hotel for a German strong point and began shelling it. The bombardment stopped after the soldiers inside located an American flag and unfurled it on the roof. Unfortunately this flag was also an excellent point of aim for the Germans and they smashed the roof and the upper story. On the night of December 17, a task force arrived and launched a strong counterattack into Berdorf, engaging the Germans in house-to-house fighting. On December 20, the Germans threw heavy reinforcements into their attack on Berdorf, the 10th Armored Division was forced back, and the Parc Hotel came under new assaults. Demolition charges blew a hole in one wall of the hotel and the order at last came through to withdraw. Even though the 4th Division had been forced to yield ground, it had blunted the attack of the entire German 7th Army for five days. We knew vaguely of this historical event, but became better informed while we were guests at the hotel. After this personal acquaintance, we studied the Battle of the Bulge in greater detail when we returned home.

Another day we visited Bastogne in southeast Belgium. In this town, also during the Battle of the Bulge, United States forces were besieged in a German counteroffensive. At one point the Germans demanded surrender, but after a very few days, the Allies began an offensive and relieved Bastogne. We were there on Memorial Day and the town was flooded with American war veterans, remembering those fights which took so many lives.

It was difficult to imagine the serene and beautifully forested Luxembourg countryside as having been the scene of such great carnage and destruction in the last half century. The battles of World War I were fiercest near here at Verdun, France. We spent a whole day visiting the forts around this city, the trenches and the endless rows of cemeteries with thousands of white crosses, many with the Star of David. For nearly two years, hundreds of thousands of the youth of France, England and Germany were slaughtered in this "war to end all future wars." Britain lost three times as many men on the first day of fighting on the Somme as she had lost in combat during the entire 22 years with France and Napoleon. The city of Verdun, despite its tremendous losses, never changed hands, due largely to the system of forts built by the French around the city, some of them still open to visitors. We saw the "Trenches of the Bayonets," where French soldiers, with bayonets attached to their rifles, were fighting when an explosion buried them. All that was visible were their bayonets, pointing out of the earth that had killed them. The soldiers were left buried with their bayonets in the trenches, the protruding points still visible today. A simple sign reads: Unknown Soldiers.

Next we visited Bitburg, the German military cemetery where President Reagan spoke on the fortieth anniversary of the German surrender. What saddened us most were the countless graves of German soldiers, many just 16- or 17-year-olds. Said Rabbi Jonathan Kendall of Santa Barbara, California, about the President's visit to Bitburg,

> "It was more than reconciliation; it was absolution, given in the name of America. The visit carried an undeniable message: 40 years is long enough; there are other drummers now, and different parades; we must get on with life and living. I hope that my heart will not, out of necessity, become hardened and inured to other acts visited upon it by those for whom history is only the past, a reservoir of events that have no bearing on the present and even less relevance for the future."

In a recent speech to the federal parliament, Richard Von Weizsaeker, President of West Germany, echoed a similar message:

> "We Germans need and we have the strength to look truth straight in the eye, without embellishment and without distortion. In our country, a new generation has grown up to assume political responsibility. Our young people are not responsible for what happened 40 years ago. But they are responsible for the historical consequences. We in the older generation owe to the young people not the fulfillment of dreams, but honesty. We must help the younger people understand why it is vital to keep memories alive."

Before continuing, he quoted the Jewish adage, "Seeking to forget makes exile all the longer; the secret of redemption lies in remembrance."

> "Today, we mourn all the dead of the war and the tyranny. In particular, we commemorate the six million Jews who were murdered in German concentration camps. We commemorate all nations who suffered in the war, especially the countless citizens of the Soviet Union and Poland who lost their lives. There is no such

thing as the guilt or innocence of an entire
nation. Guilt is, like innocence, not collective but
personal. The vast majority of today's population
were either children then or had not been born.
They cannot profess a guilt of their own for
crimes they did not commit. No discerning
person can expect them to wear a penitential
robe simply because they are Germans. But their
forefathers have left them a grave legacy. All of
us, guilty or not, old or young, must accept the
past. We all are affected by its consequences and
are liable for it. Whoever refuses to remember
the inhumanity is prone to new risks of infection."

Being reminded on this visit of the millions of human lives
destroyed in that decade, I reflected on the words of Pete
Seeger's popular song from the '60s, *Where have all the flowers
gone? Where have all the young men gone...Long, Long ago...?
When will they ever learn?*
What does it take to learn the lesson?

Lilies of the valley, blooming in Luxembourg in mid-May
1986, brought me back to my day of freedom from slavery
exactly 41 years earlier. On that warm, sunny day, I had found
those remarkable little flowers spread out under a blooming
pink magnolia tree.

To start a completely new life at age 36, I had to come alive
from an emotionless, mentally and physically handicapped
woman, to fulfill my daily responsibilities, and to be father *and*
mother to my daughter, then 7-1/2 years old. It went slowly, step
by step, with the help of my wonderful friends.

The 45-year cycle is closed. There is no beginning or end,
just as with the egg that is used as a symbol of continuing life on
the first evening of Passover, there is no interruption. There is
an event which is remembered on this Seder and told to our
children, that documents an important step from slavery into
freedom for the Jews, a few thousand years back. And the
message is, life always goes on. For 4,000 years, Jews have led an
existence which has defied logic and natural law. They have

lived and survived -- despite everything. How long will it take
until we are ready to remember the trials of European Jewry
during 12 "short years" in the twentieth century? In the words of
Rabbi Manfred E. Swarsensky at an address at the University of
Wisconsin campus in 1980:

> "The Holocaust resulted in the extermination
> of one-third of the Jews in the world as well as in
> the destruction of 1,500 years of Jewish life and
> culture in Europe. Yet the Holocaust is no proof
> that the symbiosis of Jews and non-Jews is an
> impossible dream and that the only secure future
> for Jews is in Israel. The horror of the Holocaust
> era does not prove that Jews were wrong in their
> aspiration for civic equality. It only proves that
> Fascism is dead wrong. Democracy is still man-
> kind's and the Jew's last and only hope.

> "Am I saying that the time has come to forget
> the Holocaust? Never. To forget would be a sin,
> a sin against memory, a sin against history and a
> sin against the dead. Shall we forgive? The only
> ones who could forgive, if this were possible, are
> the six million murdered.

> "But I can and will stretch out my hand and
> grasp the hand stretched out to me in recon-
> ciliation, in this as in other situations. Hatred,
> unending hatred is not the seed bed from which
> redemption can grow. I do not wish my children
> and the world's children to live forever by
> hatred. The chief task before mankind is still
> unfinished: Human beings must, at long last,
> become humane. To endure, mankind needs to
> build bridges, not walls: bridges between man
> and man, bridges between faith and faith,
> bridges between race and race, bridges between
> nation and nation."

My memories are part of me, are part of my mind and body.
They are with me constantly; no separate time must be set aside
to think and reflect. My memories are there, together with all
the love I have received and have given with a grateful heart.
The horror, the fear, the pain and the tears are also there, a part

of me that I accept without self-pity.

I want it to be known that I do not forgive anybody anything when it comes to the crimes against the Jews. It is not up to me to forgive. As Rabbi Swarsensky has said, it would be up to the six million who were murdered, if this were possible. When people call me 'too forgiving' or doubt the sincerity of my claim that I bear no hatred, I am no longer upset. I have found that arguing or even discussing this basic belief with such individuals is senseless, for they are of a one-track mind. If I am proud of anything -- and not much is there of which I can be proud -- it is that I am truly without hate or vengeance, but this does not mean that I have to love everyone.

APPENDIX
Reactions From Selected Listeners In Helen Waterford's Audiences

March 20, 1987

Dear Mrs. Waterford,

I'd like to thank you personally for coming to
our school, and sharing your experiences with
our students and staff.

In my classes today, we discussed the things
you told us, and it was evident that the students
were deeply affected and interested in hearing,
as Mr. Weichel put it, "living history". In
today's busy world, with all of the demands
on the time and interest of our young people,
it was especially meaningful to me to have one
young man say that he " wanted to cry and didn't
care that others saw it". Exposure to reality
does not come as often as perhaps it should to
kids today... you made them understand things
that had only been words in their textbooks.

I want you to know that I will do my part, as a
teacher and as a human being, to help students
remember the past so that it may not repeat itself.

The letters I'm enclosing were written spontaneously
by the students. Many wanted to speak to you, but
were a little shy at the time.

Dear, Mrs Waterford   Jan 80
thank you very much for coming
to "muir" to share your past.
with us.
     Many of us learned very valuable
lessons like when we say weve
had a rough day we think twice
about it.
     Also there are times when
I just wish I wasn't here
in the US or better yet alive.
but now when I'm in that kind
of mood I just look back
on what you told us.
     Well again I must say
thank you! for your time
and for your wanting to share
your past which I feel
will be very valuable to me
the rest of my "life"

Against such adverse and dehumanizing conditions of physical, mental, emotional, and every other kind of stress, she survived. She spoke of the death of her husband in one sentence. She did not describe to us her agony or tremendous loss in his death, or in the uncertain separation of her daughter. She simply kept emphasizing to us that <u>she</u> had to survive. She spoke from the heart about her horrifying experiences, yet, conveyed to us that the crucial ingredient for all those that did live was SURVIVAL. Victor Frankl would agree that only because they had a strong will to live did they live. The sturdy, assertive person that talked to us was down to a mere seventy pounds. (I never weighed that much growing up; I missed it.) Yet, she did not die of illness or of a faint will to live, she kept her survival need for her strength.

These past two weeks, since her lecture, I have reflected on the vile circumstances that she overcame. When any of my petty problems would surface (overdrawn at the bank, dissertation chapters beckoning, accompanying psychomatic illnesses (AKA disserationitis),stepchildren conflicts, friendships waning, piling up of laundry, filthy house. record heat, etc.) I felt grateful that I did not have to undergo any of Helen Waterford's experiences...That to be fortunate enough not to need to worry about my survival was a great gift.

What Helen Waterford is doing by lecturing to people about her experiences is a tremendous contribution to our comfortable society, in its awareness of what our human agenda is now and could be in the future.

Portion of reaction paper from a Ph.D. candidate.

The thing that touched me most about Mrs. Waterfords experience was the fact that she lived through it all, and is still sane. It's almost unbelievable. All that she has gone through is very hard for me to even imagine. I take so much for granted, and demand so much from my parents and life, that this lady's life has made me realise that I have so much to be thankful for, and that nobody really owes me anything. Especially God doesn't owe me anything. I found out that I don't have the right to complain about things. For example, I worry alot about what I'll wear tomorrow, or if my hair will look all right. I get mad at my mother if things don't go just the right way every morning. But, Mrs. Waterford hit very close to home when she said that they had to wear the same clothes for 2 months and had to get all their hair cut off. To think that they had to do all this with no choice is unreal. I tell you, I have learned a lesson. I hope that in future years I can look back on this speech and remember just how good I have it.

Portion of a letter from a Professor Peter Patschauer at Appalachian University in North Carolina, where Heck and Waterford were asked to return for a second lecture.

Your stay here was a great success. My students and I talked about your presentation in all of my classes, and they uniformly were not only impressed but also thoughtful about what they had heard and seen. It will take some more time for some of them to absorb fully what they experienced and to make this information applicable, but I think that you have again reached many a soul.

I was particulary struck by the effect you have on the women. Already after your presentation I noticed how several of them lingered around just to watch and how some others came over to talk to you, almost as if to touch you. Several of the women in my classes then said later how impressed they were by you, and I think they meant by you as a person. Here is what seems to be going on. Most of our young people hve only certain kinds of TV images that they become aware of and relate to: stars of various shows. newscasters etc. You are different in the sense that you are a star.. ja. ja. but at the same time you have and are real depth, real personality. The women especially thus find in you a person who is not only significant because of what you say but what you are. Your very presence is as significant an event in their life as your story. That is not to detract from your story. but it seems as if they are finally seeing the genuine product, a person who has experienced real difficulties and who has come through to. tell them and show them how one can live afterwards. The other thing they see is an older woman, who has real guts, real convictions and is not satisfied with quick solutions.

I am just absolutely fascinated and thrilled that you are such a wonderful example for these young women.

This is the example as it should be, a true human being . You have so much to give. Not only by telling your story, and it is truly an important one.... but by being what you are. It is so difficult to express that kind of sense or feeling I mean. Simply, there is something in the right place, what you seldom expect. It is a real inner balance and strength. One does not immediately plan to follow this example, but since you cannot escape to see those qualities one accepts the example anyway, because these expressive qualifications have a magic power one cannot resist. Amazing!

You teach without teaching and that is the ultimate art.

BIBLIOGRAPHY

Akademie der Kuenste. Buecherverbrennung Deutschland 1933, Voraussetzungen und Folgen. *Das War ein Vorspiel Nur....* Berlin-Wien: Medusa Verlags Gessellschaft, 1983.

Arendt, Hannah. *Eichmann in Jerusalem: A Report on the Banality of Evil.* New York: Penguin books, 1964.

Bettelheim, Bruno. *The Informed Heart: Autonomy in a Mass Age.* Glencoe: The Free Press of Glencoe, Ill., 1960.

Bitton Jackson, Livia E. *Elli: Coming of Age in the Holocaust.* New York: Quadrangle Books, 1980.

Blum, Howard. *Wanted: The Search for American Nazis in America.* New York: Quadrangle Books, 1977.

Borkin, Joseph. *The Crime and Punishment of I.G. Farben.* New York: The Free Press, 1978.

Borowski, Tadeusz. *This Way For The Gas, Ladies And Gentlemen.* New York: Viking Press, 1967.

Chary, Frederick B. *The Bulgarian Jews and the Final Solution 1940-1945.* Pittsburg: University of Pittsburg Press, 1972.

Cohen, Dr. Elie A. *The Abyss -- A Confession.* New York: W.W. Norton & Company, 1971.

Dawidowicz, Lucy S. *The War Against the Jews.* New York: Holt, Rinehart & Winston, 1975.

Des Pres, Terrence. *The Survivor: An Anatomy of Life in the Death Camp.* New York: Pocket Books, 1977.

Donat, Alexander. *The Holocaust Kingdom.* New York: Holocaust Library, 1978.

Donat, Alexander, ed. *The Death Camp Treblinka -- A Documentary.* New York: Holocaust Library, 1979.

Eisenberg, Azriel. *Witness to the Holocaust.* New York: Pilgrim Press, 1981.

Feingold, Henry L. *The Politics of Rescue: The Roosevelt Administration and the Holocaust 1938-1945.* New York: Waldon Press, 1970.

Fenelon, Fania. *The Musician of Auschwitz.* London: Michael Joseph, 1977.

Ferencz, Benjamin B. *Less Than Slaves: A Sequel to Hitler's Holocaust; The Story of Jewish Labor.* Cambridge: Harvard University Press, 1979.

Fest, Joachim C. *The Face of the Third Reich: Portraits of the Nazi Leadership.* New York: Pantheon Books, 1970.

Frank, Anne. *Het Achterhuis: Dagbookbrieven / June 14, 1942 -- August 1944.* Amsterdam: Uitgevery Contact, 1977.

Frankl, Dr. Viktor E. *From Death-Camp to Existentialism: A Psychiatrist's Path to a New Theory*. Boston: Beacon Presss, 1959.

Friedrich, Otto. *Before the Deluge: A Portrait of Berlin in the 1920's*. New York: Harper & Row, 1972.

Gilbert, Martin. *Final Journey: The Fate of the Jews in Nazi Europe*. New York: Mayflower Books, 1979.

_____. *Auschwitz and the Allies*. New York: Holt, Rinehart & Winston, 1981.

_____. *The Macmillan Atlas of the Holocaust*. New York: Macmillan Publishing Co., 1982.

Goebbels, Joseph P. *The Goebbels Diaries: 1939-1941.* New York: G.P. Putnam's sons, 1983.

_____. *The Goebbels Diaries: 1941-1943*. New York: Universal Award House, Inc., 1961.

_____. *The Goebbels Diaries: Final Entries, 1945*. New York: G.P. Putnam's Sons, 1978.

Green, Gerald. *The Artists of Terezin*. New York: Hawthorn Books, 1969.

Grunfeld, Frederic V. *Prophets Without Honour: A Background to Freud, Kafka, Einstein and Their World*. New York: McGraw Hill, 1980.

Haesler, Alfred A. *The Lifeboat is Full: Switzerland and the Refugees 1933-1945*. New York: Funk and Wagnalls, 1967.

Heilbut, Anthony. *Exiled in Paradise: German Refugee Artists and Intellectuals in America From the 1930's to the Present*. New York: Viking Press, 1983.

Hellman, Peter, et. al. *The Auschwitz Album*. New York: Random House, 1981.

Hilberg, Raul. *The Destruction of the European Jews*. New York: Harper & Row, 1961.

_____. *Documents of Destruction: Germany and Jewry 1933-1945*. Chicago: Quadrangle Books, 1971.

_____. *The Warsaw Diary of Adam Czerniakow: Prelude to Doom*. Briarcliff Manor, New York,: Stein & Day Publishers/Scarborough House, 1979.

Hillesum, Etty. *Het Verstoorde Leven: Dagboek van Etty Hillesum 1941-1943*. Netherlands: De Haan Haarlem, (no date).

Hoehne, Heinz. *The Order of the Death's Heads: The Story of Hitler's SS*. New York: Ballantine Books, 1966.

Hoess, Rudolf. *Kommandant in Auschwitz: Autographische Aufzeichnungen*. Muenchen: Deutscher Taschenbuch Berlag Gmbh, 1963.

Israeli Police Archives. *Eichmann Interrogated*. New York: Farrar, Strauss & Giroux; Toronto: Lester & Orpen Dennys, 1983.

Kautsky, Benedict. *Teufel und Verdammte: Erfahrungen und Erkenntnisse aus Sieben Jahren in Deutschen Konzentrationslagern*. Zuerich: Buechergilde Gutenberg, 1946.

Keegan, John. *Six Armies in Normandy: From D-Day to the Liberation of Paris, June 6 to August 25, 1944.* New York: Viking Press, 1982.

Keneally, Thomas. *Schindler's List.* New York: Simon & Schuster, 1982.

Knoop, Hans. *The Menten Affair.* New York: Macmillan Publishing Co., 1978.

Kogon, Eugen. *Der SS Staat: Das System der Deutschen Konzentrationslager.* Muenchen: Wilhelm Heyne Verlag, 1974, 1979.

Krugman Gurdus, Luba. *The Death Train: A Personal Account of a Holocaust Survivor.* New York: Holocaust Library, 1978.

Kuznetsov, Anatoly. *Babi Yar.* New York: Dell, 1967.

Langbein, Hermann. *...Nicht wie die Schafe zur Schlachtbank: Widerstand in den Nationalsozialistischen Konzentrationslagern.* Frankfurt: Fischer Taschenbuch Verlag, 1980.

_____. *Menschen in Auschwitz.* Ullstein Buch Verlag, 1973,1980.

Laqueur, Walter. *Weimar: A Cultural History, 1918-1933.* New York: G.P. Putnam's Sons, 1974.

_____. *The Terrible Secret: Suppression of the Truth About Hitler's "Final Solution."* Boston: Little, Brown & Co., 1980.

Lengyel, Olga. *Five Chimneys: A Woman Survivor's True Story of Auschwitz.* London; Granada Publishing Limited, 1947.

Levi, Primo. *The Periodic Table.* New York: Schocken Books, 1984.

_____. *Moments of Reprieve.* New York: Summit Books, 1986.

_____. *Atempause: Eine Nachkriegsodyssee.* Fischer Taschenbuch Verlag, 1982.

_____. *Survival in Auschwitz: The Nazi Assault on Humanity.* New York: Orion Press Inc., 1959.

Levin, Nora. *The Holocaust: The Destruction of European Jewry, 1933-1945.* New York: Schocken Books, 1973.

Lifton, Robert Jay. *The Nazi Doctors: Medical Killing and the Psychology of Genocide.* New York: Basic Books, 1986.

Litvinoff, Barnett. *A Peculiar People: A Fresh and Fascinating Exploration of the World's Great Jewish Communities.* New York: Weybright & Talley, 1969.

Manchester, William. *The Arms of Krupp.* Boston: Little Brown & Co., 1968.

Manvell, Roger & Fraenkel, Heinrich. *The Incomparable Crime: Mass Extermination in the 20th Century -- The Legacy of Guilt.* London: William Heinemann, 1967.

Marrus, Michael R. & Paxtorn, Robert O. *Vichy France and the Jews.* New York: Basic Books, 1981.

Mayer, Milton. *They Thought They Were Free: The Germans 1933-1945.* Chicago: University of Chicago Press, 1955.

Michel, Jean. *Dora: The Nazi Concentration Camp Where Modern Space Technology was Born and 30,000 Prisoners Died*. New York: Holt, Rinehart & Winston, 1979.

Morse, Arthur D. *While Six Million Died: A Chronicle of American Apathy*. New York: Ace Publishing, 1968.

Mueller, Filip. *Eyewitness Auschwitz: Three Years in the Gas Chambers*. Briarcliff Manor, New York: Stein & Day, 1979.

Novitch, Miriam. *Sobibor: Martyrdom and Revolt*. New York: Holocaust Library, 1980.

Nyiszli, Dr. Miklos. *Auschwitz: A Doctor's Eyewitness Account*. New York: Fawcett World Library, 1960.

Oberski, Joan. *Childhood*. Toronto: Lester and Orpen Dennys Limited, 1978.

Picker, Henry. *Tischgespraeche im Fuehrer Hauptquartier*. Seewald: Wilhelm Goldmann Verlag, 1976.

Poliakov, Leon. *Harvest of Hate: The Nazi Program for the Destruction of the Jews of Europe*. New York: Holocaust Library, 1979.

Pool, James & Pool, Suzanne. *Who Financed Hitler: The Secret Funding of Hitler's Rise to Power*. New York: The Dial Press, 1978.

Presser, Jacob. *The Destruction of the Dutch Jews*. New York: E.P. Dutton & Co., Inc. 1968/1969.

Rashke, Richard. *Escape From Sobibor: The Heroic Story of the Jews Who Escaped From a Nazi Death Camp*. Boston: Houghton Mifflin Company, 1982.

Rausch, David A. *A Legacy of Hatred: Why Christians Must Not Forget the Holocaust*. Chicago: The Moody Bible Institute, 1984.

Rosenfeld, Alvin H. *A Double Dying: Reflections on Holocaust Literature*. Bloomington: Indiana University Press, 1980.

Ross, Robert W. *So It Was True! The American Protestant Press and the Nazi Persecution of the Jews*. Minneapolis: University of Minnesota Press, 1980.

Rothchild, Sylvia. *Voices From the Holocaust*. New York: The New American Library, 1981.

Rubinowicz, David. *Dagboek, 1940-1942*. Amsterdam: A.J.G. Strengholt's Uitgeversmaatschappij, (no date).

Sachar, Abram L. *The Redemption of the Unwanted: From the Liberation of the Death Camps to the Founding of Israel*. New York: St. Martin's, 1983.

Schoenberner, Gerhard. *The Yellow Star: The Persecution of the Jews in Europe, 1933-1945*. New York: Bantam Books, 1969.

Sereny, Gitta. *Into That Darkness: An Examination of Conscience*. New York: Vintage Books, 1983.

Schmidt, Matthias. *Albert Speer: The End of a Myth*. New York: Macmillan Publishing Co., 1984.

Shirer, William L. *20th Century Journey, Volume II*. Boston: Little, Brown and Co., 1984.

_____. *Berlin Diary: An Inside Account of Nazi Germany*. New York: Bonanza Books, 1984.

_____. *The Rise and Fall of the Third Reich: A History of Nazi Germany*. New York: Simon & Schuster, Inc., 1959.

Speer, Albert. *Infiltration: How Heinrich Himmler Schemed To Build an SS Industrial Empire*. New York: Macmillan Publishing Co., 1980.

The Stroop Report. *The Jewish Quarter of Warsaw is No More!* [A facsimile edition and translation of the official Nazi report on destruction of the Warsaw Ghetto.] New York: Pantheon Books, 1979.

Thalmann, Rita, & Feinermann, Emmanuel. *Crystal Night, 9-10 November 1938*. New York: Holocaust Library, 1974.

Trever-Roper, H.R. *The Last Days of Hitler*. New York: Macmillan Publishing Co., 1947.

Thomas, Gordon & Morgan Witts, Max. *Guernica: The Crucible of World War II*. New York: Stein & Day, 1975.

Trunk, Isaiah. *Judenrat: The Jewish Councils in Eastern Europe Under Nazi Occupation*. New York: Stein & Day, 1977.

Tusa, Ann & Tusa, John. *The Nuremberg Trial*. New York: Atheneum, 1986.

Vegh, Claudine. *I Didn't Say Goodbye*. New York: E.P. Dutton, 1984.

Vrba, Rudolf & Bestic, Alan. *Escape From Auschwitz: I Cannot Forgive*. New York: Grove Press Inc., 1964.

Wells, Leon W. *The Death Brigade: The Janowska Road*. New York: Holocaust Library, 1963.

Wiesel, Elie. *Night*. New York: Hill & Wang, 1969.

Wiesenthal, Simon; Wechsberg, Joseph, ed. *The Murderers Among Us: Simon Wiesenthal Memoirs*. New York: McGraw Hill, 1967.

Wolf, Christine. *A Model Childhood*. New York: Farrar, Strauss & Giroux, 1980.

Wyman, David S. *The Abandonment of the Jews: America and the Holocaust 1941-1945*. New York: Pantheon Books, 1984.

ACKNOWLEDGMENTS

The reasons for writing my memories, my experiences, ideas and hopes are the responsibility of many, many people.

For the assistance and loving encouragement I received in helping to select a computer and overcome the fear of this "monster," I am grateful to my friend Judy Faitek.

The perfect teacher, John Gunther, instructed me with endless patience in learning to master the computer and was always available when I was seemingly lost.

The person who started me on the course I had been hoping to take for more than 30 years is my brother, Fred Katz. Our relationship is a close, warm one, and we share many ideas and ideals, but by no means all. My loving thanks for his interest in my new adventure.

My gratitude, also, to my niece, Michelle Bartlett, who gave me confidence when I was in doubt, who always was ready with valuable advice and loving support.

Eleanor Ayer, my skillful publisher/editor, has, with admirable courage, selected me to write this book. I can only hope that it was not too difficult for her to lead me through this labyrinth; I will always be grateful for this friendly push.

For the encouragement, the suggestions and the acceptance of the difficulties of living with a writer obsessed with her subject, my husband Robert can hardly be matched.

My thanks to the researchers, the reporters, writers and analysts whose names and subjects are noted herein. Without their contributions I would not have been able to put my experiences into a fitting perspective.

It is impossible to name all the hundreds of listeners across the country who expressed their feelings in personal letters to me. I have answered each one. They wrote about being impressed that I would share such personal experiences, as well as my message of hope for humanity, so that the past might serve as an everlasting memory. They were moved by my consistent love for and trust in people.